MEMORY SKILLS

THE
WORLD
BOOK

Learning Library

Volume
3

MEMORY SKILLS

Published by
World Book, Inc.
a Scott Fetzer company
Chicago

Staff

Publisher
William H. Nault

Editorial

Editor in Chief
Robert O. Zeleny

Executive Editor
Dominic J. Miccolis

Associate Editor
Maureen M. Mostyn

Senior Editor
Michael K. Urban

Writer
Sevasti Spanos

Manuscript Editor
Cynthia Fostle

Production Editor
Elizabeth Ireland

Index Editor
Joyce Goldenstern

Permissions Editor
Janet T. Peterson

Editorial Assistant
Elizabeth Lepkowski

Art

Executive Art Director
William Hammond

Designers
Tessing Design, Inc.

Photography Director
John S. Marshall

Photographers
Don Sala
Jim Ballard

Illustration Artist
George Suyeoka

Product Production

Executive Director
Peter Mollman

Manufacturing
Joseph C. La Count, director

Research and Development
Henry Koval, manager

Pre-Press Services
Jerry Stack, director
Randi Park
Sandra Van den Broucke

Proofreaders
Marguerite Hoye, head
Ann Dillon
Esther Johns
Daniel Marotta

ISBN 0-7166-3187-3 (Volume 3)
ISBN 0-7166-3184-9 (set)
Library of Congress Catalog No. 86-50558
b/hf

Contents

Acknowledgments

The diagram on page 14 was adapted from the following
publication:

Elizabeth Loftus, *Memory: Surprising New Insights Into How
We Remember and Why We Forget,* © 1980 Addison-Wesley
Publishing Co., Inc. Reprinted with permission.

Introduction

Memory plays a crucial role in your learning process. Much of what you study in school must be memorized for tests and other classroom activities. *Memory Skills* can help you improve your ability to memorize information you need to know in order to be successful in school.

The first section of the book explains the relation between your memory and learning. Basic memory aids are presented, and you are given a plan to follow while tackling all your memory tasks.

The next two sections tell you how to memorize various types of material. Section II focuses on memorizing details. Many different memory aids, such as mental pictures, chunking, acrostics, acronyms, and peg words, are given, and you can choose the ones that work best for you. Section III helps you with the difficult task of memorizing concepts by turning details into concepts and by learning the best way to memorize large amounts of material.

The fourth and fifth sections tell you how to memorize the spellings and meanings of words. Section IV gives several aids for memorizing word spellings, including special ways to deal with contractions, compound words, long words, and words that look or sound alike. Section V shows how to increase your vocabulary by using aids such as rhymes, definitions, word parts, content clues, and pairing words.

The final section of the book tells you what to do when your memory gets blocked. Some of the causes of blocked memory are explained, and methods of unblocking your memory are given.

Memory Skills can help you open doors in your mind and increase your ability to memorize and retain important information. Use the helpful hints in this book to improve your performance in school and to help your mind store and hold onto all the information you need to know.

I YOUR MEMORY AND LEARNING

This section helps you understand what your memory is, how it works, and how it affects your learning.

Your Memory and Learning

rofessor A. C. Aitken, a mathematician at the University of Edinburgh, had a remarkable memory. As part of memory tests he took in 1933 he memorized twenty-five unrelated words in a row by reading them through only twice. Twenty-seven years later, he recalled all twenty-five in the correct order without reviewing them.

The professor's memory was astounding. He asked for unrelated numbers to be given to him faster than a memory test called for. He said memorizing at the slower rate, fifteen unrelated numbers at one per second, was "like learning to ride a bike slowly." The faster rate was fifteen unrelated numbers at five per second. And he knew them forward and backward.

Professor Aitken seemed to take his memory as a matter of course and showed no obvious pleasure in it. But his associates were impressed. Aitken, for example, was a useful committee member. Whenever there was doubt about what anyone had said at a previous meeting, the professor could remember word for word. Aitken was a walking minute book.

Some experts say that anyone can develop a memory like Professor Aitken's. Whether or not that is so, it's probably true that most people can increase what they can remember by a great deal. This is important to you as a student, since memory is a vital part of your learning process. Learning is memory.

With excellent memory skills, you would have an incomparable study tool at your command. To have them, you must develop a new approach to thinking about what you are memorizing.

This section will explain what science knows about how memory works, so you can use this information to your advantage when applying the memory aids explained later in this book.

With excellent memory skills, you would have an incomparable study tool at your command.

Understanding Your Memory

Scientists have only an elementary understanding of the complex process of remembering. While some people compare memory to data stored in a computer, the process is not the same.

In a computer, data are input and stored in an electrical system via unchanging circuits. There is a limited physical space where the data are stored. The data remain there until purposely or accidentally removed from the system.

Scientists are almost certain that new human memories produce chemical changes in the brain's nerve cells and changes in their physical structure. But the changes are subtle. No one knows the location of our memories, and it seems we can't retrieve them all. Some human memory is lost with time, but we are capable of storing an indefinite amount of information.

Memory and Language Development

People start their memories at the age of four or five, and memory seems to be tied to language development. We need language to categorize and store experiences in a way that we can remember them. Examples of language memory are words and their meanings, phrases, grammatical constructions, and mathematical relationships.

Memory and Ego

Some memory changes through time. And it is somewhat self-serving and self-centered. In our memories, we often remember things in a better light. Students, for example, will remember that their classroom participation during a term was good, only to find that the teacher marked them down for failure to participate. These students are remembering what they want to, and not necessarily on purpose.

In developing your memory for study, keep in mind that you must remember accurately and struggle against your natural tendency to transform what you remember. This means among other things that you will need to review. There is no room for change when memory involves hard fact.

Mental Landmarks

A mental landmark is something that has stuck in your mind for some reason. The landmark can be a detail or an event. A detail might be the name of your first-grade teacher. You could remember that name because you repeated, or rehearsed, it so often. Or you might have been fond of the teacher. How many of your other teachers' names can you remember? How did you feel about them?

Your first plane flight might be one of your landmark events, now or in the future. You could have a "flashbulb memory" of the airplane cabin. You know how it looked, while other physical details of the trip have vanished. But the event itself and the cabin image stayed with you. Keen interest and perhaps emotion were involved.

Search your memory for its landmarks. Do they involve something you repeated many times or had a strong interest in? Probably so in many cases. Remember this when trying to develop your memory skills. You are more likely to remember something that you've repeatedly rehearsed and taken a real interest in.

You are more likely to remember something that you've repeatedly rehearsed and taken a real interest in.

Memory Wizards

Can you do this? Memorize the boundaries of every congressional district in the United States and the populations of most major U.S. cities—for different years. Then memorize the results of most of the presidential elections in the 1900's, plus the winners and losers for the vice-presidency. Impossible? One memory wizard did so just to entertain himself and his friends.

Does this memory wizard have a photographic memory—the exact memory of every detail that a person sees? No. No one has a photographic memory. It doesn't exist.

Memory wizards aren't necessarily superintelligent, either. Some people of average mental ability have fabulous memories. And so do some of low mental ability, who can remember things but not understand them at all.

Then what is the secret of having an excellent memory? That depends. Some memory wizards have an extra-good memory of what they see, keeping a long-lasting mental image of it. This type of memory comes close to what is called a photographic memory. They can describe in detail a picture they've reviewed for only a few moments. Or they can look at lists of letters or words in columns and tell you the letters or words forward, backward, across, down, and diagonally. If you ask them what the fourth word from the bottom of a column is, they can go back to their mental image and find it, out of sequence. These wizards' eyes usually move back and forth as they "read off" their mental image.

Five to 10 per cent of all children have the ability to remember images in detail, but most lose it as they grow older. Adults usually can remember details for only a few seconds after turning away from an image.

Does this mean that you are probably destined to have no more than an average memory? Not at all. In fact, having an extraordinary memory for images isn't necessarily a blessing. One memory wizard eventually had so much trouble with his mental images that he left work to become a professional theatrical memory performer. He found that the images interfered with his thoughts at work.

The key to a better memory is to develop a system for your memory tasks. Many memory wizards have nothing more than that to help them.

Three Memory Stages

Here is a diagram of your memory:

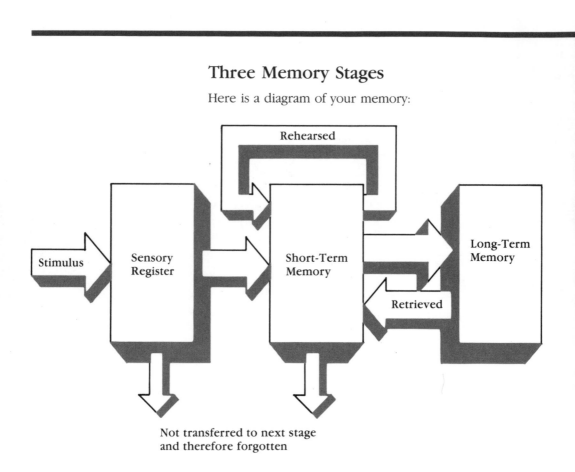

Not transferred to next stage
and therefore forgotten

Memory begins with information, called the stimulus. First the stimulus goes into sensory memory. Some information in sensory memory goes into short-term memory. From there, some goes into long-term memory. How far the stimulus goes depends on how you handle it.

Sensory Memory

When you are walking down the street, you will see many images: a street sign, a shop window, or a passenger in a car that speeds by. Most of these images will stay in your mind for only an instant. This phenomenon is called sensory memory. For the image to get into your short-term memory, you must usually transfer it rapidly through concentration. Otherwise, it is lost.

In terms of school studies, how you handle sensory memory is important. If you glance just once at the example your teacher has jotted on the board, you may never remember it. The same goes for what the teacher says. An explanation will "go in one ear and out the other." Your teacher's understanding has not transferred to you. And that's a permanent loss.

Short-Term Memory

Most of us have at some time looked up a telephone number, become distracted, and had to look up the number again because we'd forgotten it. What we did in this situation was put the number into our short-term memory by concentrating on it for a few seconds. Since information in short-term memory lasts only about twenty seconds unless we keep concentrating on it, the distraction erased the information from our thoughts.

You are concentrating to keep information in your short-term memory when you keep repeating a phone number to yourself as you walk from the telephone book to the phone. After you stop repeating the number, its memory fades until it is gone. If you keep concentrating on the number, you can keep it in your short-term memory indefinitely. If you use a number frequently, like your own phone number, the 55-mile-per-hour speed limit, or the TV channels available to you, you will remember them for years. These numbers have become permanently stored in your long-term memory and can be retrieved.

Your short-term memory can hold a few items at a time. In retrieving, the better your long-term memory knows an item, the less likely you are to confuse it and the less you have to concentrate in short-term memory.

People can knit, hum, and rock at the same time, keeping track of the stitch, tune, and beat all the while. Most of us routinely dance and talk, plus enjoy the music. All of these activities involve memory. Think about it. At different times you memorized how to knit, hum, rock, dance, talk, and recognize a tune. You memorized by storing information in your long-term memory. You can bring it back whenever you want and use the different skills simultaneously.

The longer you think about something, the more likely it is to go from short-term memory into long-term memory. If you need a piece of information to do well at school, be sure it's well stored through practice.

Long-Term Memory

You can think of short-term memory as the top of a desk. Long-term memory is what's inside the drawers. You can sense what's in your short-term memory. But you cannot sense all your long-term memory. You look at it in pieces, through your short-term memory. You bring long-term memory back to act on something, like a test.

Your long-term memory is the biggest part of your memory. It is nearly limitless. Long-term memory holds information that is a few minutes old or many years old. Some information, like mental landmarks, goes into your long-term memory without special effort.

Much of the information you need to succeed in school goes into your long-term memory when you deliberately try to memorize it. Since there is no limit to the amount of material you can remember, saying you have too much is no reason for poor school performance. In cases like this, your problem probably is that you are going about your memory task wrong.

The way and enthusiasm with which you respond to a memorization task determines what you will remember and the extent to which you will remember it. You can probably improve your long-term memory if you respond in an effective way.

Your long-term memory is the biggest part of your memory. It is nearly limitless.

Memory Measures

Think of how it would be to wake up each morning having to memorize everything all over again. Not only couldn't you talk or think, but you couldn't walk, eat, or do almost any other kind of mental or physical activity.

Many scientists are fascinated with how we remember. They test the development of our memories from childhood through advanced age. They know, for example, that in a series, we best remember the items at the beginning and the end. We remember the middle items less well. So, if you are trying to remember:

6,8,3,6,1,9,3,7,4,2,9

you have to give special attention to memorizing the middle numbers. Try it.

Scientists also know that we remember odd items before ordinary ones, no matter where in a series an odd item appears. Try:

8,3,9,4,2,psst,7,5,6,9,4

What do you remember best from this series?

Generally, we also need to concentrate on the less-than-remarkable fact. Everyone knows who George Washington is. Do you remember anything about Franklin Pierce?

Why and to what extent we forget is a subject in itself. Most of our long-term memory stays with us, under normal health conditions, until death. Under hypnosis, people have brought back extraordinary memories that they were unaware of while conscious.

But often, under normal circumstances, we can't bring everyday memories back. Have you ever had a strong feeling that you knew someone, but couldn't be sure? Or has someone's name been on the tip of your tongue, only to stay there and embarrass you? What is the extent of these "memories"? What can you do if you experience "feeling-of-knowing" and "tip-of-the-tongue" problems during a test? You'll find out in this book.

There are three ways to measure how much a person remembers: recall, recognition, and relearning. Scientists use all three. So do teachers, in their evaluation of your school progress.

Recall

Recall is your ability to remember something off the top of your head. When you complete a teacher's short-answer, fill-in, or essay test item, you usually have to recall all the information. None of it is supplied.

Recognition

When, by consulting a list, you are able to pick out the correct names of state capitals, you are remembering by recognition. It is easier to recognize than to recall. For this reason, students perform well on multiple-choice and matching tests, where the teacher has them associate an assortment of information they can see.

Relearning

Relearning means to learn again after you have forgotten something. Our memories tend to drop details. But most people memorize information faster if they have already memorized it once.

If you have kept up with your studies, you relearn when you review for end-of-chapter or end-of-term exams.

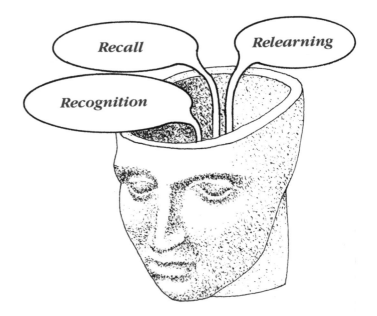

The more you put into memorizing during daily study, the greater your advantage in relearning for big tests.

Storing and Retrieving

Memory is the librarian of your brain. A librarian puts materials away according to a system. Then, when someone wants the materials, the librarian knows where to go to get them back. The librarian stores and retrieves materials. These are also the main activities of your memory.

In terms of your school success, retrieving might cause you more anxiety than storing, since retrieving has to do with your performance in class. There are times when you know you've stored information well but still can't get it back into your thoughts for a test, no matter how hard you try. And, while a librarian might be sure that a book is "somewhere on that shelf," you really have no idea where your memory has gone. You might be anxious that it isn't in there at all anymore, though it most likely is.

Memory Aids

Since people began to think, they have devised memory aids to help them retrieve memory. Students seem to make up memory aids automatically.

Some memory aids are inside of you—you carry them around in your head. Examples are rhymes, like the spelling rule "*i* before *e* except after *c*." Others are outside your mind, like lists.

The best advice for boosting your memory is to use as many inside and outside aids as you can to memorize anything. The more attention you pay to the information, and the more ways you work with it to make it your own, the more likely you are to remember it.

Memory aids force you to develop cues that jog your memory. Many cues for a single piece of information increase your chances of remembering it. Let's look at inside and outside memory aids and the kinds of cues they give you.

Inside memory aids. Inside memory aids might go everywhere with you, but you must first memorize them and often make them up yourself. That takes time and work.

These aids tend to set your memory because of the demands they place on your creativity and attention. Constructing an aid fixes information in your mind that could remain there long after you have forgotten the aid itself. Besides rhymes, inside memory aids include substitute words, mental pictures, and combinations of the two. These are inside memory cues.

An acronym is a substitute word. If you wish to memorize the names of the Great Lakes, think of HOMES—*Hu*-ron, *O*ntario, *M*ichigan, *E*rie, and *S*uperior. Here you have used the first letter of each lake's name to create an acronym that is a familiar word you can remember easily. Students have used this acronym for many years to cue the names of the Great Lakes.

While we have some catchy rules, acronyms, and other word systems that people have taught us to use, most of the time we have to create our own mental pictures. Say you want to remember what formed the Great Lakes. Picture the acronym HOMES above a glass. Glaciers formed the Great Lakes. The glass cue associated with the acronym

Superior   Huron   Ontario

Michigan   Erie

will jog your memory of glaciers because the first three letters of *glass* and *glacier* are the same and because the consonant sounds *s* and *sh* are close. To remember that glaciers are made of ice, fill the glass with ice.

Linking is important when developing inside memory aids. You linked HOMES, a glass, and ice to memorize the names of the Great Lakes and information about how they were formed. Another example of linking that doesn't use a mental picture is to memorize that the telephone was invented in 1876 by remembering that 1876 is 100 years after the signing of the Declaration of Independence.

Outside memory aids. Outside memory aids include lists, outlines, notes, flashcards, and other props with written cues. These aids are excellent for memorizing and, as with inside aids, your attention to constructing them sets the memory of the material in your mind.

Overlearning

Overlearning takes place when you memorize information over and over again, long after you can recall it perfectly. Time is an important factor in overlearning. If you think you know the Preamble to the Constitution by heart, set it aside for two hours. Then try to recite it again, and again two hours later. Repeat the exercise the next day, and the next, perhaps increasing the amount of time between repetitions. Overlearning assumes that you can never memorize anything too well.

Memorizing on Location

Say you are trying to memorize the steps in a procedure for a science experiment you will demonstrate in class. You could put the steps in an outline and try to memorize them while working at your kitchen sink and stove, perhaps with glasses instead of test tubes.

But you would do much better to arrange with your teacher to practice the procedure in the school lab. Not only will you have the advantage of working with the school equipment that you will use the day of the demonstration, but also all the room cues will be familiar.

We recall better in locations where we originally memorize material.

We recall better in locations where we originally memorize material. The lab's features will increase rather than block your memory because they were part of your memorizing environment. These cues include not only the equipment, but also the lighting, noises, furniture, and other features of the room.

You can take this strategy a step further. If you are trying to memorize the French terms for parts of an automobile, take a list of the terms, with their definitions, and practice them in your family's car. You can't take an automobile to a test. But you have increased your available memory cues, and these are your pathways to recall.

Building Memory on Memory

Memories build on memories. Look at this stanza from Lewis Carroll's nonsense poem "Jabberwocky," from *Through the Looking-Glass:*

> 'Twas brillig, and the slithy toves
> Did gyre and gimble in the wabe:
> All mimsy were the borogoves,
> And the mome raths outgrabe.

This poem is utter nonsense, but it is easier to memorize than this nonsense:

> Brillig and 'twas toves slithy the
> In gyre wabe the did gimble and:
> Borogoves mimsy the were all,
> Raths the and outgrabe mome.

Carroll's stanza follows the English speech pattern that you have memorized to form sentences. It also rhymes, which your memory understands.

The second stanza, which line for line has the same words, follows no pattern at all. The second stanza would be difficult for most people to memorize.

From your memory's viewpoint "Jabberwocky" makes sense of nonsense. That's why it's easy to learn. You need to make sense of your lessons to memorize them. And they are perfectly logical, which puts you a step ahead for starters.

In general, the more familiar something is, the more likely you are to memorize it. Bring what you know into memory with the information you are trying to memorize. Create direct associations between what you know and what you have to memorize, such as using the cue HOMES for naming the Great Lakes, or knowing when the telephone was invented because it happened 100 years after the signing of the Declaration of Independence.

Bring your own originality, interests, and techniques to any memory task.

Look for cues within the subject matter itself. Then, if you want to further improve your chances with aids such as memorizing on location, add them to your memorization activities.

Customizing Your Memory Aids

You must take information in accurately in order to remember it accurately. But the best way for others to take it in might not be the best way for you. Bring your own originality, interests, and techniques to any memory task.

Originality

Pi has fascinated mathematicians for thousands of years. Pi is the ratio of the circumference of a circle to its diameter. When written as a decimal, pi has no pattern that repeats, as does, for example, the decimal equivalent of 1/3 (0.3333333 . . .). We can take pi, whose close fractional equivalent is 3½, or ²²⁄₇, to a specific number of decimals, like 3.14159265, or we can keep going forever: 3.14159265358979. . . .

You are more likely to remember items that you respond to in a novel way that is comfortable for you. A. C. Aitken, whom you read about at the beginning of this section, could recite the first 1,000 decimal places of pi without error. He learned 802 places in 15 minutes. With his incredible recall, perhaps he needed no special memory aid. Others do.

You are more likely to remember items that you respond to in a novel way that is comfortable for you.

Here's one aid for remembering pi's first four decimal places:

Yes, I know a number.

The number of letters in each word are memory cues that translate into 3 and the digits of the first four decimal places: 3.1416. Just remember to put in the decimal point and ignore the period at the end. Here's another aid for pi:

May I have a large container of coffee?
3   1   4   1   5   9   2   6

This is 3.1415926. The fourth decimal place is 5 because it isn't rounded, as in the first example. Now try this:

Pi

Pie.
I wish I could determine Pi
Eureka cried the great inventor
Christmas Pudding Christmas Pie
Is the problem's very center.

The letters in each word equal the first 20 decimal places of pi. Note that the first word in this aid cues the 3 before the decimal.

Try original solutions in your memory tasks. But don't make memory aids more complicated than the task itself. If you can't remember the aid, it won't help you.

And don't waste your precious study time memorizing something of no use to you. If all you need to know is the first two decimal places of pi, you probably don't need any memory aid. It isn't hard to remember 3.14 without using a cue.

Interest

Advertising uses memory-jogging techniques to make us remember products so that we will purchase them. Take a look at the ads on TV or in magazines. They are full of catchy phrases, unusual images or motions, and bright colors. All these are designed to appeal to our interests and hold our attention.

When you're memorizing for school, frequently you have to stimulate your own interest. You will naturally prefer some subjects over others. Find things in your subjects that make you want to learn about them. If you are weak in history, but enjoy getting to know people, approach memorizing historical figures by reading about their personalities, lives, problems, and challenges. If you'd like to know about technology, find out how the people lived— look up information about their homes and transportation, for example.

And build interest-getters into the memory aids you use. On flashcards, use bright colors. For mental pictures, think of images that will stick with you—perhaps amusing ones. Make your rhymes peppy, not dull. Your memory aids are your own. No one else has to see or hear them. Have fun with them.

Expand or Contract?

There are two basic ways to develop memory aids. You can either expand or contract information you need to memorize. One way is as good as the other, depending on how you wish to think about the information.

Suppose you wish to remember the spectrum colors: red, orange, yellow, green, blue, indigo (a dark, grayish blue), and violet. You could expand the information by making up a sentence. The first letters of each word in the sentence would be the first letter of each color:

Rosalind only yesterday grew better in vamoosing.

This type of memory aid is called an acrostic.

To contract, you could make up an acronym with the first letters of each color: ROYGBIV. To remember this acronym better, group the letters to form a name: ROY G. BIV.

Mental pictures can be expanded or contracted. If you want to remember that penicillin was discovered by Alexander Fleming, expand with mental pictures that link two cue-images at a time. Picture a penny on a window sill (*penicill*). Then forget the penny and picture a sill in a flame (*sill in flame,* for *cillin* and *Flem*). Next, forget the sill and see a flame spurting out of an inkwell (*flame* and *ink* for *Fleming*). To contract, just picture a penny in a flame. Then you have the cues for the beginning of *penicillin* and *Fleming.*

Notice that the mental pictures in the expanded aid are not linked together by any kind of story. They stand on their own. A story would only complicate the memory aid needlessly. And while this aid is good for remembering things in order, it won't help you memorize anything out of order. But there are other aids for that.

Matching Aid to Task

The right memory aid for you depends on the way you think and the task at hand. Let's say you are preparing for an essay test. You are going to have to recall information on your own and make connections between ideas. One way to tackle this problem is to make an outline of your material and pick out the key topics. Express them in only one word. Then create acronyms using the first letter of each word.

Suppose you will write an essay about explorers in the New World. You have studied your text and notes and made your outline. You understand the importance of the people you are reading about and their exploits. But you need some memory cues for the details.

The explorers are Columbus, Ponce de León, Cortes, Cartier, and Coronado. You're unlikely to forget Columbus, so concentrate on the others.

Use the first letters of the explorers' names to spell an acronym: POCOCACORN (*Po*nce, *Co*rtes, *Ca*rtier, *Co*ronado). You need the *r* and *n* from Coronado to distinguish him from Cortes. To remember what nations they represented—Spain (Columbus), Spain, Spain, France, and Spain—think of four S's and an F. Remembering that Cartier is French is easy—his first name is Jacques, and Cartier is not a Spanish name. Your memory aid is POCOCACORN, four S's and an F. These cues, plus your understanding of the information in your outline, should get you through the essay.

On the other hand, you might be studying for an objective test with matching items. Perhaps you have to memorize dates for these explorations—1492, 1513, 1521, 1534, 1540—and match them to the explorers.

Again, we all know Columbus. He came to the New World first, in 1492. Use that as a base. The other explorers came later, in the 1500's. Their dates have the first three digits ascending: 151, 152, 153, 154. Use POCOCACORN to keep the explorers in order. Now add TOF-0 for the fourth digit in the dates (three, one, four, zero—1513, 1521, 1534, 1540). Your memory cues are POCOCACORN TOF-0. That's all you need, plus Columbus.

Understanding—The Key Aid

When you memorize, never leave understanding out. It's your best memory aid.

Our educational system emphasizes learning through understanding, with good reason. Look at the memory aids you just read about. POCOCACORN TOF-0 is gibberish. It will do you no good in the long run if you don't understand the importance of the explorations, which is what your lesson was really about. When you memorize, never leave understanding out. It's your best memory aid.

Rote Learning and Memory

Rote learning occurs when you memorize word for word or number for number. Often we learn by rote because we are expected to recite something. Rehearsing by repetition is an important part of rote learning.

Rote is especially useful in memorizing poems, which have the built-in memory aid of rhyme. But how long do you think you'd remember these lists if you memorized them by rote?

Columbus	Spain	1492
Ponce de León	Spain	1513
Cortes	Spain	1521
Cartier	France	1534
Coronado	Spain	1540

Generally, avoid learning large amounts of material by rote unless your teacher wants you to recite. And, even then, make sure you understand the meaning behind the material. Then you can appreciate what you've taken so long to memorize and use the ideas behind it to build more memory later.

Memory Tricks

Memory tricks are as varied as your imagination. You have already seen a number of them, such as acronyms, acrostics, and mental pictures. There are several benefits to selecting these as aids.

The tricks make you less dependent on rote learning, which can be dull and short-lived. And they increase the chance that you will recall and recognize information, which is important to any student. This builds your confidence and motivation. Having some tricks up your sleeve will make you less nervous. And you tend to remember more when you are calm.

Developing memory tricks forces you to plan. You have to organize your material well and spend quite a bit of time making up and learning the memory aids for it. Organization and time spent on any memory task increase your chances of remembering.

Mental images and word associations are a big part of memory tricks. Both are excellent memory joggers. And you put familiar things in memory tricks, like a glass or a common word like *homes*. You memorize what's in a familiar context faster than what's not.

When devising and using the tricks, you must pay attention—a necessary part of good memorization. The tricks are also interesting, which improves your willingness to memorize. And the more you practice the tricks, the more you process the information. This increases the chances that it will go deeply into your memory.

There are some perils in using memory tricks. Some won't appeal to your way of thinking. On occasion, they take longer to make up and memorize than it takes just to memorize the material by rote. And, if used with no understanding, memory tricks short-change your education.

Keep in mind that memory tricks can help you memorize faster but don't necessarily make you remember things longer. The degree of memorizing, not the speed, is what counts. Even though nonsense takes a long time to memorize, for example, if you learn it well, you don't forget it any sooner than meaningful material. It might not be particularly useful, but you remember it.

Your memory is not a muscle. You can't bend and flex it to make it strong. That's why memory aids probably don't strengthen memory, but they do help you remember better because of the effort you invest in them.

You will become acquainted with many memory tricks in this book. By all means, see if you can adapt them to your memory tasks, but don't think they're something they are not. They will give you a boost, that's all. Understanding will give you security.

Motivation and Memory

Motivation is an important memory aid.

Motivation is an important memory aid. Whenever you have a memory task, whether you are memorizing details for a quiz or concepts to carry throughout your life, get a good grasp on why being able to recall the information is important to you. Memorizing will be drudgery if you make it so. But it can also be fascinating.

Setting Goals

Your goals depend on your motivation. Are you memorizing mathematics symbols to get a D instead of an F? to stay on a team? to get a private phone your parents promised you in return for a good grade? What happens to what you have memorized when you achieve these short-term goals?

Lasting memory takes interest. If you fail to view your memory task as an important part of your overall learning goals, the information might not sink deeply into your mind. You can relearn the information if you need it again, but you might have to do so almost from scratch.

Having a Plan

When you face any task, the first—and perhaps most important—step is to draw up a plan to achieve it. Here is a basic plan for all memory tasks:

1. Understand what you are to memorize, even if you have to do extra research.

2. Make up a schedule. Give yourself plenty of time.

3. For each memory session, get in the right frame of mind. Think only of the memory task at hand.

4. Select your memory aids. Don't try to memorize while you do so. Figure out the best strategies first, memorize later.

5. When you begin to memorize, concentrate.

6. Don't rush. Memory takes time.

7. Overlearn—review the information and the aids again and again, never assuming your memory is perfect.

II MEMORIZING DETAILS

This section presents various methods for memorizing different types of details.

ACROSTICS

PEG SYSTEMS

ROTE

CLUSTERS

Memorizing Details

arry Lorayne, a memory wizard, has an extraordinary memory for detail, even though he was unable to finish high school and says he has an average IQ. He's demonstrated his skills on nationwide TV. When introduced to an audience of up to 500 persons, he can remember all their names. Lorayne says he doesn't need an address or telephone book. He keeps names, numbers, and addresses in his head.

This section is going to show you many aids for tackling memory tasks that involve detail. No one aid is best for every task. Pick and choose among the aids according to how easy each is for you to use. Never use one that confuses you.

You can apply these aids to information outside school, like memorizing phone numbers and addresses. In fact, this is a good way to practice using them.

But don't go overboard memorizing details. If you're learning how to prepare footnotes and bibliographies, for example, you usually don't have to remember every kind of information that belongs in them and the correct order of presentation. Instead, refer to your text, notes, or a stylebook. This is what these references are for. But do remember that they are there to use.

Memory by Rote

Rote memorization is the least efficient memory aid. Most people with ordinary memories cannot remember rote-learned information for very long. But it is useful when you have only a few details to memorize. Rote learning also works when the material has built-in memory cues of its own.

Rehearsal is an important part of rote learning. Make sure to schedule plenty of time for it.

Rote with No Aids

If you have been studying the colonial period in American history, you should be able to remember that there were thirteen colonies, settled mostly by the British. Names like the Pilgrims, Plymouth Rock, and Pocahontas are details that stick in your mind by rote without any special memory aids. And they will probably stay there due in part to how often you have American history through the grades.

Rote by Rhythm and Rhyme

That Columbus's three ships were the *Niña,* the *Pinta,* and the *Santa María* can easily be learned by rote because their last letters rhyme. Rhythm and rhyme are built-in memory aids.

When memorizing rhymes and poems, especially short ones, use rote if you wish. Try this one:

> In civics class,
> Sue took one note.
> That's all she knew
> 'Cause that's all she rote.

For years, children have memorized how many days are in each year with "Thirty days hath September, April, June, and November. . . ." It's fun to create rhymes and poems of your own as memory aids. Here's one for remembering the three planets closest to the sun:

> Mercury's closest to the sun,
> Earth is the third closest one.
> The beautiful planet in between us
> Is the goddess we call Venus.

Rote by Tune

In addition to rhythm and rhyme, tunes have music, which is also a good memory aid. Do you recall the ABC's song that children sing? It goes to the tune of "Twinkle, Twinkle, Little Star" and ends with "Happy, happy we will be, when we learn our ABC's."

Let's use the tune of "Twinkle, Twinkle, Little Star" to memorize some geometrical figures and the number of sides they have. Just fit these words into the tune:

Triangles have 3, no more,
Quadrilaterals have 4,
Pentagons have 5, just 5,
Hexagons add 1 to 5.
Pyramids are strange to see.
They have 4, but you see 3.

Rote with Games

Games are good for fixing information in your memory.

Games are good for fixing information in your memory. You work with other people, which keeps you alert. Games are also competitive, which makes them interesting. Interest spurs memory.

Adapt your memory tasks to games when you can. There are a number of educational games for sale. But here's a free game called Buzz. Use it to memorize the multiplication facts.

You can play this game when you're walking home with friends. You need three or more people to play. The example uses the multiplication facts for 7.

Start clockwise. The first person says 1, the next person says 2, until you get to 7. The person who is to say 7 says "buzz" instead. Then go counterclockwise. The person next to the one who said "buzz" says 8, and the cycle continues until you get to 14. The person with 14 must say "buzz." Repeat the process. Keep going until you get through the multiples of 7. Repeat for any numbers whose multiples you want to memorize.

Rote and Rewrite

Generally, writing something over and over is a poor memory strategy. Not much sinks in. There are two exceptions to this. One is rewriting words to memorize their spelling, both in English and in other languages. You will learn more about rewriting to memorize spelling later in this book.

The other exception occurs when explaining things to yourself will help you memorize them. Then you should write down your explanations so you can review them.

Say you are trying to memorize the name of a treaty, like the North Atlantic Treaty. You will memorize it better if you understand it and can describe it in familiar terms like these:

> The North Atlantic Treaty came after World War II (1949). It created the North Atlantic Treaty Organization (NATO) to defend Western nations. NATO is in charge of the defense, which the nations work together to achieve.

You should be able to see that this is easier to understand than a textbook description:

> In 1949, the North Atlantic Treaty provided for the collective defense of Western nations by the establishment of the North Atlantic Treaty Organization (NATO).

Sometimes you have to remember the significance of a symbol, piece of art, or other image. Say your art teacher wants you to remember what impressionism is. Here's a definition:

> A style of painting developed by French painters of the late 1800's that gives the impression made by ordinary subjects on the artist without much attention to details. The painters used dabs or strokes of primary unmixed colors to reproduce how light actually reflects.

This definition will not stay with you unless you tie it into something that has meaning for you. Select an impressionist painting that you will picture whenever you think of impressionism, perhaps *At the Milliner's* by Edgar Degas. Describe it and write down your description:

> This painting shows an ordinary French woman at a hat shop. The clothes are from the late 1800's. There is nothing unusual about what the woman is doing. Most of the colors are blues, yellows, and greens. There's a bright red hat in the picture. The lighting looks like it's sunlight from a window, reflecting off the people and objects in the room.

From now on, when you think of impressionism, you will get your memory cues from this picture: ordinary scenes, late 1800's, primary colors, natural lighting reflected off objects in the painting.

Inside Joggers

Inside joggers are aids you have committed to memory that remind you of materials you want to be able to recall. They allow you to remember lots more than rote, and in split seconds.

These joggers will take longer for you to read about than to use. Be patient going through the explanations. Read them carefully and practice each aid that appeals to you.

Some of these memory aids are verbal—that is, you can jot them down. Find out before any test whether your teacher minds if you jot your memory aid on your test or a piece of scratch paper after the test has begun.

Mental Pictures

Most people know the shape of Italy. It is shaped like a boot. In French, the English Channel is called *La Manche,* which means *the sleeve,* because it is shaped like a sleeve.

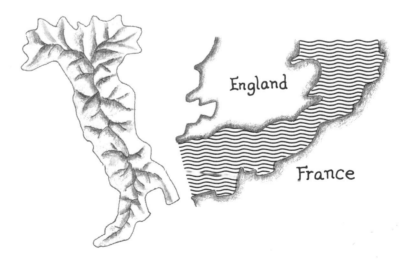

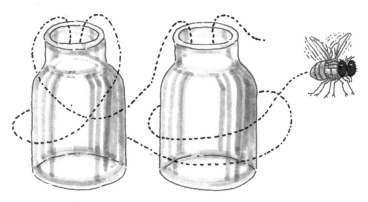

Mental pictures help us remember things, as long as the pictures are crystal clear. Suppose you can't remember what a preposition is. Think of two bottles and a fly. A fly can go around, above, behind, between, inside, into, or within the bottles, and beneath or under the bottles if you pick them up. All these words are prepositions, whose functions you remember with a mental picture that explains how they work.

This example shows how a mental picture can help you memorize an abstract idea—the function of prepositions. But mental pictures are usually easier to use in remembering concrete items, such as names and objects. If you are trying to remember that Jacob Perkins was an American who invented the refrigerator, for example, picture a parking (Perkins) lot filled with refrigerators.

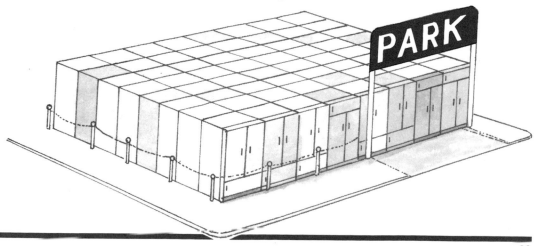

PARK

Some memory experts say that the stranger the mental picture, the easier it is to remember. It's up to you. Would you remember that Perkins invented the refrigerator more easily by imagining a stove-top refrigerator with a spout, perking coffee? Then use it.

Chunking

Chunking means memorizing material in small groups, which are easier to memorize than long strings of numbers or words. You chunk when you memorize a telephone number, like this:

1-312-555-4325

instead of this:

13125554325

Try memorizing this number, with and without chunking:

88459530286

You can also abbreviate and chunk. Suppose you want to memorize the thirteen executive departments of the United States government. They are the Departments of State, Treasury, Defense, Justice, Interior, Agriculture, Commerce, Labor, Health and Human Services, Housing and Urban Development, Transportation, Energy, and Education. You may memorize these in any order. Start with the departments that have more than one word in their names:

HHS HUD

Now make up words from the rest of the letters:

DISTAL EJECT

As a result, four small chunks will bring an enormous amount of memory back to you:

HHS HUD DISTAL EJECT

Remember that your short-term memory can hold only a few items at a time. When you bring back chunks, you are holding more in your mind if they represent a lot of information, and you can handle the information more easily. The same principle holds when you are paying for something, say a pack of gum that costs 30 cents. It's easier to pay with three dimes or six nickels, and they are easier to handle than 30 pennies.

Renaming

Renaming involves finding a familiar word to stand for an unfamiliar one in order to jog some details out of your memory.

You can use this aid to remember names. Shylock is the Shakespearian character who suggested cutting off a pound of flesh from someone as payment for a debt. Change Shylock to Shylimb, and you will be able to identify him. Shakespeare's Banquo was a ghostly guest at a banquet. Change his name to Banghost to memorize it.

You can also use this technique to remember names

that go together. If you want to remember that the legendary characters Romulus and Remus founded Rome, combine their names to Romremus. For Scylla and Charybdus, two sea perils Odysseus had to pass through in the *Odyssey,* think Scyllibdis.

Don't let these combination words influence your spelling. They are just for helping you recall. If you are a poor speller, you might decide not to use this aid. But if you are a good speller, go ahead.

Key Words

The key-word method involves finding a word that sounds like a word you want to memorize and linking it to a mental picture. It works excellently for memorizing foreign vocabulary and also for many other memory tasks.

The German word for fork, *Gabel,* sounds like *gobble. Gobble* is your key word. Picture someone gobbling with a fork. Then, to recall *Gabel,* remember *gobble* and see the picture.

Do you have trouble remembering in what direction parallels and meridians go? When you see meridian, think of a merry-go-round with the poles holding the seats going up and down, vertically. Meridians go vertically. If you know what meridians look like, you know that the parallels go the other way—horizontally.

     Do you want to memorize national capitals? For Poland, whose capital is Warsaw, picture a pole with large eyeglasses looking at a battle (*pole saw war,* or Warsaw).

To memorize scientific descriptions, which can be hard to rewrite in familiar terms, write down your information in groups of three sentences, with the main definition first:

1. The candela is light's measuring unit.

2. It is the part of the electromagnetic spectrum you can see.

3. The amount of light emitted from a candela or other luminous source in a given period of time is measured in lumens.

Make up a key word to represent the key concept in the first sentence: *candle*. Add key words for the other two sentences and picture a lighted candle on a magnet with an electrical cord plugged into a loom.

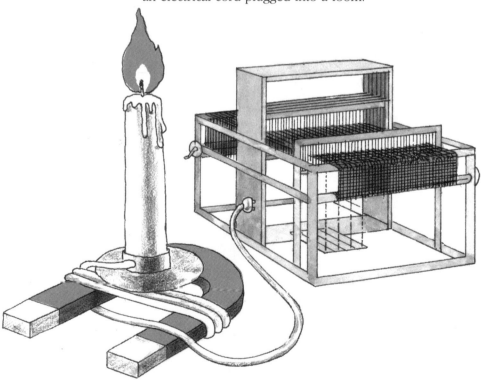

You have three images to represent each of the three sentences. The candle is the main image. If you understand your material, this should be enough to bring back your memory of its description.

Linked Sentences

Putting concepts in sentences and linking the sentences is a good way to remember information. Say you want to memorize the names for the major climate types: tropical, subtropical, temperate, boreal, polar, highland, and dry. Use rhyme, alliteration, and any other language devices to remember the sentences better and make their links easier. The example below uses alliteration, and the last word in each sentence cues the first word in the next. The sentences can make sense or not, according to what works best for you. These do not:

Putting concepts in sentences and linking the sentences is a good way to remember information.

Tropical types taste subs.
Subtropical types sometimes swallow temper.
Temperate types talk boring.
Boreal'd best be polite.
Polars back peanuts high.
Highland has hardly dried.
Dry. (No link needed for the last item in a series.)

First-Letter Cues

Using the first letters of words as memory cues is a time-worn but excellent memory aid. First-letter cues are useful when you have a strong feeling that you know something but can't remember it. You use first-letter cueing when you can't remember someone's name and start going through the alphabet to see if one of the letters will jog your memory. Have you ever done this to remember a name on a test? Try it. It works.

Acrostics

Music students have memorized "*E*very *good boy does fine*" for years to remember the notes on the treble clef:

EGBDF. This kind of first-letter memory aid is called an acrostic. Here's a variation:

> My! Vicki earned more just selling used neckties, Pete.

The first letters of the words in this example represent the names of the nine planets in our solar system in order from the sun: Mercury, Venus, Earth, Mars, Jupiter, Saturn, Uranus, Neptune, and Pluto. You can't mix up Mercury and Mars with this aid. *M* and *y* (*My!*) are the first and last letters in *Mercury*. *More* has the first and third letters in *Mars*.

This technique works for math, also. If you want to remember the formula for the perimeter of a rectangle ($P = 2l + 2w$), use this sentence:

> Poems are 2 long and 2 wordy.

Poems stands for *perimeter, are* signals the equal sign, *2 long* stands for *2l, and* signals the plus sign, and *2 wordy* stands for *2w.* If you're memorizing several perimeter formulas, always use *poems* for *P, are* for = , and *and* for + .

Acronyms

Acronyms are excellent memory aids.

You can expand or contract in first-letter cueing. "Every good boy does fine" expands EGBDF into a sentence. ROY G. BIV contracts the colors of the spectrum colors into an acronym.

Acronyms are excellent memory aids. Say you want to remember the eight parts of speech: noun, pronoun, adjective, verb, adverb, preposition, conjunction, interjection. There is no need to remember them in this order, so change the first letters around to form an acronym that you can remember: PAVINPAC.

Sometimes you will have to memorize real acronyms as part of your lessons. Take DNA, or deoxyribonucleic acid, "the substance of which most genes are made and that is chiefly responsible for the transmission of inherited characteristics." All you really need to remember is that DNA is the most important determiner of heredity. Expand DNA into an acrostic: *Darn near another (baby).* You'll remember the acronym and what it pertains to.

Memory Pairs

Sometimes you must memorize things in pairs. Or you might decide to put things in pairs to memorize them. Make verbal and picture associations between the items. Always see if they have anything in common and use that in the aid.

You can memorize most of the German pronouns by pairing them with English pronouns. Here are English/German pronoun pairs in the nominative case:

I/ich
du/you
es/it
wir/we
sie/she

That just leaves *er* (*he*) and *ihr* (plural *you*)—not too much to memorize by rote.

If you have to memorize which states the Presidents came from, first write down the Presidents and their states in pairs. Examples are George Washington/Virginia and Franklin Roosevelt/New York. Using a key word for Washington, picture a washtub on the verge (Virginia) of a cliff. For Roosevelt, see a rose standing in an egg yolk (New York).

Continue through your President/state word pairs, using *verge of a cliff* for Virginia and *yolk* for New York with key words for the other Presidents who came from those states. How about James Monroe from Virginia or Martin Van Buren from New York? Now try Presidents from other states: Ulysses S. Grant from Ohio, Dwight D. Eisenhower from Texas, and John F. Kennedy from Massachusetts.

Clusters

Clustering, or placing things in categories, is a strategy that allows you to memorize things in smaller groups.

Clustering, or placing things in categories, is a strategy that allows you to memorize things in smaller groups. Clustering is a highly effective memory strategy because it forces you to discriminate. That takes concentration, which sends the memory deeper into your mind.

You can cluster many ways, including alphabetical order, size, and function. Let's say you must memorize the independent nations of South America. Alphabetically, they are: Argentina, Bolivia, Brazil, Chile, Colombia, Ecuador, Guyana, Paraguay, Peru, Suriname, Uruguay, and Venezuela. You can try to memorize them in alphabetical groups of three:

Argentina	Chile	Guyana	Suriname
Bolivia	Colombia	Paraguay	Uruguay
Brazil	Ecuador	Peru	Venezuela

If you don't find that easy, chunk the first letters:

abb, cce, gpp, suv

You might be able to recall the first-letter chunks more easily. The first three chunks rhyme, and an acronym, *suv,* ends the series.

You can also cluster these countries by relative size after checking their statistics and locating them on a globe to fix their size in your mind:

Huge	Big	Medium	Small
Brazil	Peru	Venezuela	Guyana
Argentina	Colombia	Chile	Uruguay
	Bolivia	Paraguay	Suriname
		Ecuador	

By size, your chunks for first letters are:

ba, pcb, vcpe, gus

Ba and *gus* are easy to remember. That leaves only *pcb* and *vcpe,* and you can develop your own memory tricks for them if you don't want to use rote.

Sometimes information is in a hodgepodge, like these math symbols:

$$< \rightarrow \times = + \therefore \leftrightarrow \geq \div - \neq \leq \cdot \pm - >$$

Cluster them according to function:

Add or subtract	plus sign ($+$), minus sign ($-$), plus or minus sign ($\pm$)
Multiply or divide	times ($\times$), times ($\cdot$), and division sign ($\div$)
Show less or more	is greater than ($>$), is less than ($<$), is greater than or equal to ($\geq$), is less than or equal to ($\leq$)
Lines	line ($\leftrightarrow$), line segment ($-$), ray ($\rightarrow$)
Results	equals ($=$), is not equal to ($\neq$), therefore $\therefore$

After sorting the information this way, you should be able to memorize it much more easily.

Peg Systems

People have been using peg systems to memorize for over 300 years. Peg systems consist of numbers or letters associated with words. Often mental pictures are used with peg words.

You can do extraordinary things with peg systems once you memorize them, including remembering, out of order, dozens of items in a series. This isn't true of the key-word, first-letter, and some other aids you are learning about.

To use a peg system, you first memorize its peg words. Once you do, they're a real short cut to memorization, especially for concrete terms. Pegs, however, aren't particularly useful for memorizing abstract terms or several lists. Other aids are better for that.

Peg systems can be difficult to memorize and take practice. Anytime a peg system becomes more difficult to memorize than the material you have, abandon the system. Find another way to memorize your material instead.

Rhyming Peg Words

One peg system pairs numbers with words with which they rhyme, like 1 and *bun*. This is a peg-word list that uses that strategy:

1 bun

2 shoe

3 tree

4 door

5 hive

6 sticks

7 heaven

8 gate

9 line

10 hen

Here is a list from 1 to 10, with the rhyming peg for each number, the most populated nations of the world in order, and a symbol to associate with each nation. You will use the symbols in mental pictures. (The symbols have to make sense to you. If you find these difficult to remember, make up your own for this example.)

1. (bun) China, rice

2. (shoe) India, cow (sacred cow)

3. (tree) Russia, bear

4. (door) United States, eagle

5. (hive) Indonesia, Indian

6. (sticks) Brazil, brazil nut

7. (heaven) Japan, geisha girl

8. (gate) Bangladesh, empty bowl (poor)

9. (line) Pakistan, pachyderm (elephant)

10. (hen) Nigeria, Niagara Falls

To remember that the United States is the fourth largest nation, when you think United States, picture an eagle over a door, which combines the mental picture with the United States and the rhyming peg for 4. To remember that Nigeria is the tenth, see a hen rowing a boat over Niagara Falls. Try making up some of your own pictures for this list. Use odd images like the last one if you find them effective for you.

If you want to change the peg words, go ahead. And they don't have to rhyme. Memory experts use nonrhyming peg words, as you shall soon see. Perhaps they'll work for you, also.

But never try to link your mental pictures into a story sequence. That will just confuse things. Your objective in using these pegs is to be able, off the top of your head, to say which item ranks where, not to list the items in order. Use other aids for that.

Alphapegs

You can use the alphabet as well as numbers to develop a peg system. If you're using a number system and an alphabet system, you have to take care not to confuse the peg words from each set. Practice your peg words well.

Alphapegs are used like number pegs. Since you probably don't know the positions of the letters (1–26), you can't use alphapegs as easily for a series. But you can count the alphabet's letters off on your hands for short lists. And the alphapegs have other uses.

Alphapegs can either rhyme with the letters of the alphabet they represent, begin with the first sound of the letter, or both. Here's one list that mixes the two:

a = ant
b = bee
c = ceiling
d = door
e = eel
f = fort
g = goose
h = house
i = isle
j = jar
k = coat
l = ladle
m = mouse
n = knot
o = owl

p = pear
q = quill
r = rat
s = sail
t = towel
u = uke (ukulele)
v = veil
w = wrist
x = Xmas (wreath)
y = yarn (ball of yarn)
z = zipper

Say you want to remember the formula for the area of a trapezoid:

$$A = \tfrac{1}{2}h(b_1 + b_2)$$

With alphapegs, think:

> An ant [A] looking at [=] half a house [h]; half a house [$\tfrac{1}{2}h$] next to a corral [( )]; a corral [( )] with one beehive at left (b_1) and [+] two beehives (b_2) at right.

If you have a short list, remember it with alphapegs. Suppose you want to remember the list of the first thirteen states to join the Union:

a. Delaware

b. Pennsylvania

c. New Jersey

d. Georgia

e. Connecticut

f. Massachusetts

g. Maryland

h. South Carolina

i. New Hampshire

j. Virginia

k. New York

l. North Carolina

m. Rhode Island

Use key words for the states, plus mental pictures that the alphapegs provide—for example, a farmer (in the dell) with an ant on his head for a., Delaware, and a pen in a beehive for b., Pennsylvania. Try finishing the rest of the pictures. You might want to use the key words for Virginia (on the verge of a cliff) and New York (egg yolk) that you saw in the earlier section on key words. It's always good to keep your memory cues as standard as possible.

Alphapegs are also useful for memorizing spelling. See the spelling section for suggestions on how to use alphapegs this way.

The Phonetic System

People have been using the phonetic system to aid their memories since the mid-1600's. This system is similar to but more versatile than the peg system and is excellent for memorizing numbers.

For this aid, you group the consonant sounds in ten categories, associated with numbers 1 through 10. The categories contain sounds that are produced in the same manner and are close in pronunciation. For example, *z, s,* and soft *c* are formed by putting the front teeth together and forcing out air. They sound much alike and are grouped together for number 10. *K, q,* hard *c,* hard *g,* and *ng* are all formed in the back of the throat. They are grouped for number 7.

Here are the consonant sounds that correspond to numbers 1 through 10 and the reasons for putting the numbers and consonants together.

Number	Consonant	Reason
1	*t, d, th*	*t, d* have one downstroke
2	*n*	*n* has two downstrokes
3	*m*	*m* has three downstrokes
4	*r*	*r* is the last sound in the word *four* in several languages
5	*l*	*L* is the Roman numeral for 50
6	soft *g, j, sh, ch*	*G* resembles a 6; backward script *j* resembles a 6
7	*k, q,* hard *c,* hard *g, ng*	*k* can be combined with 7; or *k* is two 7's
8	*f, v, ph, gh*	8 and script *f* both have two loops
9	*b, p*	upside-down and backward *b* or backward *p* resembles a 9
0	*z, s,* soft *c*	*z* is the first letter of *zero; c* is the first letter of *cipher* (0)

With this code, any number can be converted into a word or a sequence of words made up of consonant sounds that correspond to their numbers. Use no more than two consonants per word for beginners.

Suppose you need to remember that the population of the United States is over 233 million. With this code, that translates into *no ma'am*. Under 234 million is *no more*. Here's another one: There have been 40 U.S. Presidents—*Rahs!*

Albert Einstein announced his theory of relativity in 1915: *Dab tile*. Add a mental picture: a mad scientist in a lab coat dabbing tile in the bathtub.

Notice that the vowel sounds don't count at all in this peg system. Sometimes all the consonants in a peg word don't count either. The sounds of the consonants are what matters. *Judge* is the equivalent of 66, not 616. The *d* is not pronounced. In *cough,* the *gh* counts as an *f. Cough* is 78.

You can split up any number to memorize it with this system. Then link the words for each split with mental pictures (but don't link them into a story).

An example is 7,759,647,401. Here you have the words *cake* (77), *lap* (59), *chair* (64), *crow* (74), and *seed* (01). To remember, visualize a cake with a lap. Blank that picture and see someone's lap with a chair on it. Blank that picture and see a chair being carried away by a crow. Blank that picture and see a crow eating a seed. If you can remember the first picture, a cake with a lap, you can remember the number.

If you'd like to practice the phonetic system, go through some numbers to see if you can come up with words for them. Here are some: 1 is *toe,* 11 is *toot,* 21 is *knot,* 101 is *toast.* Try some more.

Phonetics and Peg Words

Some people associate the phonetic system with unrhyming peg words like these:

1   *t,* toe

2   *n,* knee (pronounced *nee*)

3   *m,* mow

4   *r,* ray

5   *l,* lei

6   *j,* jay

7   *k,* key

8   *v,* view

9   *b,* boa

10   *s,* sow

Those well trained in the system can use peg words for numbers over 100:

150 = dolls
200 = noses
250 = nooks

If you practice this system enough, you will know a number instantly by the peg word you associate with it.

Finding long words to represent big numbers is challenging but fun. Did you know that the height of Yosemite Falls is *doormouse* (1,430 feet) and that *totalitarianism* is really 11,514,203? See if you can find some more.

Plotting Points

Around 500 B.C., a Greek poet named Simonides is said to have left a banquet hall just before the roof collapsed and killed everyone else there. The victims' bodies were so badly crushed that their relatives were unable to identify them.

Simonides did, it's reported, by remembering where everyone had sat. Thus he became the inventor of a popular method, which we will call plotting points, to remember the sequence of topics for speeches. The method can also be used for memorizing items in a list, in or out of order.

Plotting points is good for temporarily memorizing a list of concrete items that are easily pictured. You can often use the same points for different lists. But you should memorize only one list with your locations at a time. If you have more lists, use another string of points.

Points to Write By

Plotting points is good for temporarily memorizing a list of concrete items that are easily pictured.

When plotting points for a written test, you have to picture locations you know well, such as the classroom or your home. Your points at home might be your front walk, the stairs to your porch, the porch itself, the screen door, the inner door, and the living room couch. You picture the items in your list at each point. Some people are successful at picturing more than one item at a point.

A good thing about plotting points is if you forget one item at one location, that won't prevent you from remembering another item at another location. There is no linking from item to item. But you can't automatically remember the number of an item in a list unless you count the points off. If you have used your locations a long time, of course, you might know the number.

Make sure that the item you are remembering contrasts well with the location you are putting it on. One memory wizard reported that, when memorizing his grocery list, he made the mistake of plotting an egg on a white wall. Later, when he tried to remember what he had associated with the wall, all he could see was white.

Say you want to remember the sequence in which plant life appeared on earth. On your front walk, picture a pine cone (cone-bearing plants). On the stairs, picture a daisy (flower-bearing plants). On the porch, picture grass. On the screen, picture a wheat shaft (grains). On the inner door, picture an apple (fruit). On the living room couch, picture corn (cultivated plants).

Points to Speak By

For speeches or oral reports of any sort, become acquainted with the room in which you will present. Say you are doing a report on karate. The topics are:

How old karate is
How religious leaders started karate
How karate came to America
How war further acquainted U.S. soldiers with karate
How karate relies on kicks
How "karate" means "empty hand" because no weapons are used

You are meeting in a regular classroom. Pick out your points in that room beforehand and fix an image for each topic on each point, going from left to right or right to left:

door—an old man
flag—a Buddhist monk
blackboard—Uncle Sam
back door—a cannon
table in back of room—a mule
window—a hand with the palm facing you

You can put in a quote or two, if you find a concrete item to stand for it and a point to fix it on. But you will probably have to memorize the quote by rote.

For speeches or oral reports of any sort, become acquainted with the room in which you will present.

These days, people usually have aids like cue cards for talks and speeches. But plotting points is still useful when no aids are allowed.

Story Chaining

A Russian memory wizard memorized this formula in seven minutes:

$$N \cdot \sqrt{d^2 \times \frac{85}{VX}} \cdot \sqrt[3]{\frac{276^2 \cdot 86x}{n^2v \cdot \pi264}} \, n^2b \;=\; SV\frac{1624}{32^2} \cdot r^2s$$

He made up this story to do so:

> Neiman (N) came out and jabbed at the ground with his cane ($\cdot$). He looked up a tall tree that resembled the square root sign ($\sqrt{}$), and thought to himself: "No wonder the tree has withered and begun to expose its roots. After all, it was here when I built these two houses (d^2). . . . Then he said, "The houses are old, I'll have to get rid of them ($\times$); the sale will bring in far more money." He had originally invested 85,000 in them (85). . . .

This story continued four times longer, until the memory wizard got to the end of the formula. He could recall the formula fifteen years later, with no advance warning.

Story chaining is good not only for single lists or formulas, but for several. You can make up as many stories as your mind can hold for a test. For essay questions, you can chain topics you want to cover—just list them in order for each essay first. Unique stories work well.

Story chaining is good not only for single lists or formulas, but for several.

This example is from math. You have two formulas to memorize, both having to do with basic properties of real numbers:

commutative property of addition

$$a + b = b + a$$

While commuting (commutative), Applecheeks (a) and ($+$) Bartholomew (b) knew they could reverse ($b + a$) seats.

associative property of addition

$$(a + b) + c = a + (b + c)$$

Because of their close association (associative), Applecheeks (a) and ($+$) Bartholomew (b) were hemmed in [( )], but added ($+$) a friend, Cornflakes (c). The result was ($=$) that Applecheeks (a) had time to be alone, and ($+$) Bartholomew (b) and ($+$) Cornflakes (c) got hemmed in [( )].

If you have a number of formulas to memorize, keep the same words for the same mathematical symbols and functions. Applecheeks can always be the variable a, with Bartholomew b and Cornflakes c. *And* can always mean *plus*, and *hemmed in* can always mean *put parentheses around*.

Let's apply this memory aid to a list. You want to memorize the ten brightest stars. They are, in order, Sirius, Canopus, Alpha Centauri, Arcturus, Vega, Capella, Rigel, Procyon, Betelgeuse, and Achernar. Here's the story:

> The movie stars (stars) looked serious (Sirius) opening the can of punch (Canopus). They were hungry and decided to all send for (Alpha Centauri) food. As poor actors (Arcturus), they had come to Las Vegas (Vega) hoping for a couple of (Capella) good meals. But they ordered rye jelly (Rigel), protein (Procyon) wafers, and a bottle of juice (Betelgeuse). They ate everything at a nearby (Achernar) park bench.

This story won't help you to spell the names of the stars, but it will cue their names and help you with their pronunciation.

If you have a number of formulas to memorize, keep the same words for the same mathematical symbols and functions.

Outside Joggers

People use outside, or external, memory joggers when they tie a ribbon on their finger or wear their wrist watch on the wrong wrist to help them remember something. Outside memory aids students can use are flashcards, cue cards, tapes, sights, sounds, and other sensory experiences. You can't take outside joggers everywhere with you, but they do help set details in your mind.

Flashcards

You can put flashcards together quickly. All you need is some index cards, a pen or pencil, and, sometimes, glue. You can make flashcards for any subject and use them over and over.

For math, use flashcards to memorize the fractions and their decimal equivalents, or to memorize the conversions from standard to metric forms.

In literature, you can put the names of books on one side of flashcards and the names of their authors on the other. Or you can put the names and authors on one side and brief plot summaries on the reverse. Then, alone or with a partner, you can read either side and describe the reverse until you've memorized the card thoroughly.

Try whenever possible to practice your flashcards with a partner. The task will be more like a game that way, and you'll keep your interest up.

You can adapt flashcards to practice inside memory aids. When you are memorizing foreign words, put a key word and picture for the word on one side and the appropriate foreign word on the other. Or, for any subject, put first-letter cues on one side and what the cues represent on the reverse. An example from science is the acronym PROMETANATEL, which cues the four stages of mitotic cell division: *pro*phase, *meta*phase, *ana*phase, and *telo*phase.

Color helps us remember things. Use color on your flashcards to highlight something you might forget. For example, if you were having trouble remembering to put the cubed sign on this formula for the volume of a sphere:

$$V = 4/3 \ \pi r^3$$

you could color the ^{3} red for emphasis.

> *Color helps us remember things. Use color on your flashcards to highlight something you might forget.*

Cue Cards

Cue cards are used for speeches, oral reports, and other oral presentations. You jot down important words on them and then use them as memory cues when you talk. For an oral report on John Quincy Adams, you might write these cues on the card:

(Cue)	Information to Be Recalled
6th	sixth President
1824	election year
John Adams—2	father, 2nd President
Federalist	belonged to Federalist Party
Jackson	disputed election, Jackson got most electoral votes
4	served only four years, unpopular President
Rep	served in House of Representatives after left presidency
gag	gag rules, which Adams fought against in Congress
1848	died of stroke while serving in House

Experience

You will probably prefer to use different senses for different kinds of memory tasks. But you should try to use them all as much as possible. Most people understand the value of sight to memory. But memory based on hearing may be better. Studies have shown that what you hear tends to stay with you longer than what you see.

Many foreign languages have masculine and feminine nouns. Examples from French are *le visage, the face* (masculine), and *la langue, the tongue* (feminine). There are some rules that can help you guess which nouns are masculine and which are feminine, but there are so many exceptions, you would do better just to memorize the articles (*le, la*) with the nouns. Take advantage of your ability to memorize through hearing by saying the articles with their nouns aloud, many times, until they naturally go together.

Taping your voice and playing it back is yet another aid to memorizing through hearing.

Taping your voice and playing it back is yet another aid to memorizing through hearing, in foreign languages and other subjects. In chemistry, you can tape the names of the elements and leave a pause during which you recite their symbols (actinium, Ac; aluminum, Al; mercury, Hg).

This forces you to concentrate because you have only so much time to come up with the symbol.

Don't shortchange any of your senses—that includes touch, taste, and smell. If you are skeptical, how many times do you think someone has to touch a cactus to remember that its needles are sharp? Did you ever chew down on a raw piece of garlic by mistake, and would you again? Do you know what sulfuric acid smells like when someone tells you it has the odor of burning eggs?

Use your senses on field trips. If you are going on a field trip for geography, for example, participate. Don't just take notes. If you are trying to memorize a habitat's features, see them: Are the plants sparse or bushy? Touch them: Is the ground slimy or hard? Smell them: Are the flowers scented or not? Hear them: Are there birds chirping or bees buzzing? Taste them: Is water in a stream brackish or sweet? (Make sure it's safe to taste first.) These characteristics will register in your mind as strong memory cues to reinforce anything in your textbook or notes.

> *Use your senses on field trips. If you are going on a field trip for geography, for example, participate.*

Math Aids

Is math particularly difficult for you? Do you do it quickly and accurately? If not, part of the problem might be that in grade school, you never memorized some basic math material, such as the addition, subtraction, multiplication, and division facts. That $6 + 8 = 14$ should be automatic to you by now, as well as that $8 - 6 = 2$, $6 \times 8 = 48$, and $48 \div 6 = 8$.

If you haven't memorized the math facts for 1 to 10, there are some special memory tricks in this section that will help you do so. There's also one for the 11's and for some geometry facts.

In the future, use these aids and any others you've learned to memorize the basic measurement equivalents, the squares of common numbers, the decimal equivalents of common fractions, and the formulas for perimeter, area, and volume. If you haven't already had these, they are coming up in your curriculum. Memory builds on memory, especially in math. Once you've caught up, don't slip behind again. For top math performance, you'll at least need instant recognition of math facts, basic measurement equivalents, and the decimal equivalents.

Use Your Fingers

Children often count on their fingers. But did you know you can also multiply with them? Here's how to use them to memorize the multiples of 9 or to check them instantly.

Stretch out your fingers and thumbs in front of you and imagine they are numbered 1 to 10, from left pinkie to right pinkie. Curl down the left pinkie (1). The number of fingers left is 9, or 9 × 1. (Count thumbs as fingers.) Put the pinkie back up and curl down finger 2. You have 1 finger to the left (pinkie) and 8 to the right. That equals 18, or 2 × 9. Keep going, and you will see that with each finger you curl up, you are left with 27, 36, 45, 54, 63, 72, and 81—the multiples of 9.

For 8's, use a modified version of the 9's technique. Try 3 × 8. Curl down your third finger and you get the answer for 3 × 9, or 27. Now subtract the multiplier, 3, and you get the answer for 3 × 8: 24.

The 11's are easy up to 9 × 11—you just write down the multiplier twice: 2 × 11 = 22, 5 × 11 = 55. Here's a memory aid for multiplying 11 by 10 to 18. Add the digits of the multiplier and put the total inside the multiplier: 12 × 11 = 132 (1 + 2 = 3, put inside 12 = 132). When multiplying with a number over 18, carry the 1. For 57 × 11, add 5 + 7 = 12. The answer is 627. You've added the 1 in 12 to the 5 in 57 and placed the 2 in the middle.

Use Props

Marbles, Buttons, Pebbles, or Pennies

Props are good memory aids in math. In fact, some child geniuses taught themselves math with props. George Parker Bidder taught himself to calculate with marbles and buttons. André Ampère used pebbles.

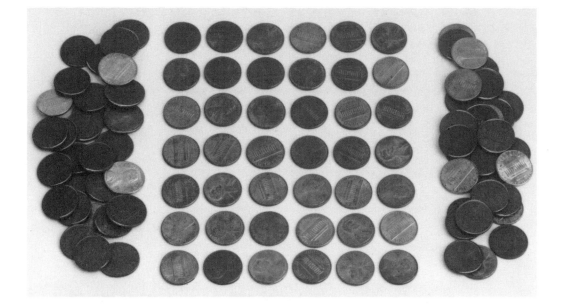

Pennies are just as useful, and abundant. If you need to memorize the facts for 1 to 10, get 100 pennies. The next aid will illustrate how to practice the multiplication and division facts for 7 with pennies, but you can adapt the technique to the other operations and numbers.

Put 70 pennies in a pile (7 × 10 = 70, and we aren't going past 10). If you want to know 6 × 7, put seven pennies in each of six groups and you will have 6 × 7, or 42 pennies total in the groups. Count them. With seven groups, you have 7 × 7, or 49 pennies total. With eight, you have 56.

Now go backward for division. With 56 pennies in a pile, to find out what 56 ÷ 7 is, put the pennies in seven groups, one by one. You'll have eight pennies in each group when you're through (56 ÷ 7 = 8).

Use this technique to practice the multiplication and division facts for all the numbers that give you trouble. Notice that in the examples you were also practicing addition to check the answers. Vary the technique to suit yourself and you can also practice subtraction.

Cardboard Figures

If you are trying to memorize the properties of geometric figures, build some. For triangles, make an equilateral, a scalene, an obtuse, and a right triangle from hard cardboard strips. Fasten the ends. Try to push any of the triangles, changing the angles. They won't budge. Not only have you fixed the shapes of these triangles in your mind, but you have a memory cue for one of their properties. Triangles are rigid. This is why they are often used in architecture: they provide solid support.

Now construct a square the same way. Push it. It moves, forming a parallelogram. Do the same for a rectangle. You have memorized that four-sided figures are not rigid. Are their angles congruent? You should be able to figure out and memorize that easily with this aid.

III   MEMORIZING CONCEPTS

This section presents some memory aids that will help you remember concepts.

Memorizing Concepts

Robert A. Lovett, a former U.S. Secretary of Defense, has an incredible memory. Once, for a law school exam, he quoted a legal case line by line, including the numbers. If you've ever seen any legal cases, you know what complex pieces of writing they are. Reading the Constitution of the United States or a contract will give you some idea of what legal writing is like.

Lovett's professor didn't know what to think. He called the student in. Lovett was faced with getting an A or a zero. He got out of the tight spot by reproducing the case by rote all over again. He got his A, but his experience has meaning for you as a student. Through his answer, Lovett showed incredible rote-memory powers but not his understanding of the case. Rote reproduction wasn't what his professor was expecting, and it isn't what your teachers want. They are looking for your understanding of the concepts behind what you are learning.

A concept is a general thought. "Roundness" is a concept in math. You understand roundness by seeing or touching round objects, like circles or spheres. In grammar, "verb tense" is a concept. When you understand the differences between *I am*, *I was*, *I will go*, and *I will be going*, you know the concept of verb tense.

Concepts stay with you a long time, once you've mastered them. They are lifelong companions that bolster memory. They give you a frame of reference for understanding new material. And when you forget details, understanding concepts helps you know which ones are missing.

This section presents some memory aids that will help you remember concepts. Many involve review. Also included are strategies for memorizing large amounts of material, which is easier to do when, as a part of your daily study, you emphasize the concepts that hold the material together.

Turning Details into Concepts

Concepts and Review

Details can be confusing. And they lead to false assumptions. Take this example. You have memorized that in German *gross* means *big*. You start to study French, and you find that *gros* in French means *big*. One detail helps you remember the next. This is called a positive transfer of learning.

Soon you come to the French word *gras*. You remember that in German, *Gras* means *grass*. You assume *gras* in French means *grass*. Wrong—it means *fat*. This is a negative transfer of learning, which you must guard against.

In foreign language study, you sometimes start out by memorizing details like words and definitions, perhaps by rote. But you also should say the word in sentences for review, and repeat the sentences until the word's meaning sinks into your memory with the language's sentence patterns. This is how you memorize a word's usage. Usage is a concept. You can't memorize usage by rote.

You should further review by learning how to read the word in context so that you understand the grammar associated with it. Grammatical relationships are also concepts.

There's no excuse for using *gras* for *grass* in French. *Gras* is not a noun. It's an adjective, and most adjectives don't function the same as nouns, in any language. Try saying "The fat is green," or "That lady is grass." Nonsense in English, nonsense in French. If you've memorized the concepts that govern this word's use, you will never make this kind of mistake.

When you review your lessons, you in effect glue together everything you have memorized. Concepts are mental glue. In American history, for example, you may have memorized that Lincoln, Johnson, and Grant were the 16th, 17th, and 18th Presidents, plus details of what happened when they were in office. Through review, you can start to understand the differences among their administrations and the effects one had on another. These are concepts,

Concepts stay with you a long time, once you've mastered them.

built from detail, and they will stay with you long after you've forgotten that Lincoln, Johnson, and Grant were the 16th, 17th, and 18th Presidents.

To grasp concepts during review, you need to focus on general ideas. If you are memorizing details that you didn't take the time to learn earlier, you will get hung up on individual facts and never reach the concept level. When the details fade, your memory won't have concepts to back you up.

Concepts and Interest

Real interest in your subjects will help you memorize the concepts that underlie them.

Real interest in your subjects will help you memorize the concepts that underlie them. But no one can help you develop this memory aid. You have to develop interest on your own. Here's an example of how to go about it.

You've started algebra. At first, it doesn't interest you particularly. You know nothing about algebra, so why should it? You struggle to pay attention in class.

You start memorizing details like variables and signs for operations, and soon you know enough to make connections in your thinking—you're developing concepts. They interest you, particularly since they start to make other details—new vocabulary, formulas, and operations—quicker and easier to memorize. The lessons become like puzzles to solve, rather than confusions of letters and numbers. And you like puzzles.

By keeping up with the details of algebra at the beginning, you mastered its concepts, first because they were useful, and then because they were interesting. You've avoided having trouble memorizing both the details and the concepts of algebra.

Concepts and Participation

Participation is important in all memory tasks, including concept learning. At the end of the last section, you saw how to increase your memory of math details by making models of geometric figures. Did you realize that you were memorizing concepts at the same time?

From making a cardboard triangle, you memorize that a triangle has three sides and three angles. These are details. But when you try to move the sides and can't, showing that the figure is rigid, you memorize the concept of rigidity. And you've done so far more effectively than through a definition in your textbook.

Participate actively in memorizing concepts. Put your own interests into them. When you are reading literature, for example, try to understand why the author wrote the book. What are the author's points of view? What have they to do with the way you live and think? These are concepts. The book might eventually influence your thinking. If so, you can bet you'll carry its concepts past graduation.

Memorizing Large Amounts of Material

You've seen many special memory aids and strategies. Now it's time to look at how to pull together some basic techniques when you find yourself responsible for memorizing a large amount of material.

When faced with large amounts of material, think about where you are in relation to your memory task. If you're starting from scratch, you'll have a difficult time. But, if you have kept up with your studies, you shouldn't be facing this predicament.

Your teachers know that learning in general and memorizing in particular are better done over a period of time, in short amounts. This is why they prepare lesson plans and present lessons gradually across a set time span—a grading period, a term, or an entire school year.

Don't thwart their efforts. Your best aid to memorizing large amounts of material is to keep up with your studies. If you fall behind, the best advice is to spend as much time as possible catching up.

Class Presentations

You have learned that you often remember what you hear longer than what you see. Listening in class, whether to your teacher or to other students, is an important memory aid that can make a big difference when you cover large amounts of material.

You are much more likely to recall a good teacher's explanation of a science principle like photosynthesis than your textbook's explanation—if you really pay attention. The teacher will explain the process several ways, and each way is a different memory aid for you to recall later. You can ask questions, which forces you to deal with the process in your own words. And you can listen to your classmates' questions, which forces you to deal with photosynthesis in their words.

Students' presentations, like extra-credit reports or experiments, can be as useful as the teacher's. Often, the topic is important, or it wouldn't merit a special report. Don't use someone else's report as a time to relax. Concentrate to store some additional memory cues.

Note Taking

Note taking improves memory when you organize and save your notes.

Note taking improves memory when you organize and save your notes. Just jotting down what someone says won't help. You can write down and recopy a definition a hundred times and still not have it memorized. If you don't understand it, you won't remember it.

Reorganize the details into logical patterns. You'll remember them better if you work with them this way. Soon the concepts that hold the points together will be obvious. And you'll have the reorganized notes to review for big tests.

Reading for Memory

Reading itself isn't a good memory aid. Reading with attention and an effective plan is. These steps will help you remember what you read and organize large amounts of reading material.

Prereading

At the beginning of any reading assignment, review the entire selection. Store its memory cues in your mind: contents list, chapter title, subheadings, introductions, summaries, and questions or exercises. These parts of the text will show you many of the details you have to memorize, plus the concepts that you must develop by reading the selection.

If you are reading a chapter on pronouns, start by reading about what a pronoun is. You'll probably find that in the introduction. Then look at the headings: Personal Pronouns, Relative Pronouns, Interrogative Pronouns, Demonstrative Pronouns, Indefinite Pronouns. As a result, you know that you have five different kinds of pronouns to understand. Read the end-of-chapter summary. It will probably tell you, in brief terms, the differences among the pronouns. Then look at the exercises you have to do.

By the time you start reading, you will already have memorized quite a store of details about pronouns, and you will be able to anticipate explanations of the lesson's concepts. The text will make more sense to you, and what makes sense to you is easier to remember.

Reading

Read More Than Once. One rule of thumb in reading for memory is to plan to read material more than once. But space your reading. Reading something twice in one night is not so good for your memory as reading it twice but two days apart. Rereading at the end of a term is especially good for memorizing, since so much time has passed since the first reading.

Recite. While rereading is effective for memory, recitation is even better. Recitation in this context doesn't mean saying exactly what is written. It means repeating what the text says in your own words, which will help you remember anything.

If you can't reword a sentence because you don't understand it, ask for help from your family or teacher. The passage will start to make sense to you. If for some reason by the end of a unit or term a passage still baffles you, master it then. But don't let it slip by. It probably has important concepts that are escaping you.

Underline. Memory comes from response. Color makes things stick in your memory. Respond to key ideas in your reading by underlining them in color. Later the underlining will also help you organize the details and concepts into the lists or outlines that you'll need for review.

Summarize. Summarize each paragraph in your own words as you read it. Then, when you finish with the entire selection, summarize all the paragraphs again. You will force concepts and details deeper into your mind, they will last much longer, and you'll recall them more easily.

Outline and List. When you have finished a selection, outline the key ideas. The outline will suggest the connections between the ideas, and you will begin to understand how the concepts are woven together. At the same time, make lists of details you think you'll need to memorize. Keep the outlines and lists for review.

Stars

I. Stars in the Universe.

A. How many stars are there?
B. The Size of stars.
C. The Distance of stars.
D. Why Stars Shine.
E. Color, temperature, brightness.
F. Star motions.
G. Star groups.

II How people use the stars.

A. Measuring Direction and position
B. Measuring Time
C. Learning from the Stars.

III Kinds of Stars.

A. Main-Sequence Stars.
...d Super giant.

Diagram. Take the key ideas from the selection and put them in a "cue tree." Use the branches for the key points, and twigs coming off the branches for related, lesser points. Or put the main topic in a circle in the center of a piece of paper and let the supporting points radiate from it. Making diagrams like these will fix concepts and details in your mind. Keep the diagrams with your outlines and lists.

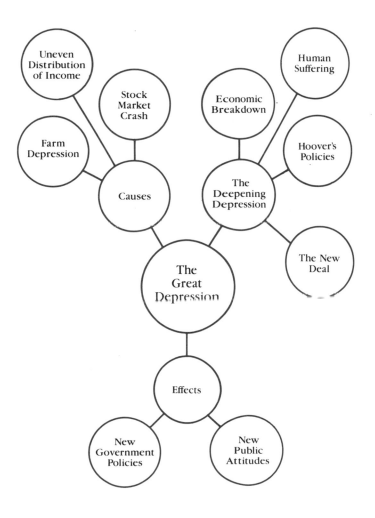

Handling a Big Review

Bring Materials Together. When you're dealing with large amounts of material, much time passes between the start of memorization and the time for review. Thus, a big review involves relearning. To make relearning easier, bring together everything you used to memorize when you originally studied the material. This includes special memory aids, notes, outlines, lists, diagrams, and books.

Schedule. Draw up a schedule for your review. You memorize better in short sessions. Make sure you space your memorizing across several days.

Know the Evaluation. How you memorize might depend on how you will be evaluated. Find out if your teacher is going to try to gauge your recall, your recognition, or both. For recall, you will have to remember information on your own. For recognition, the teacher will provide some aids.

For essays, your recall of both concept and detail are tested, but concepts can be more important. You cannot write a good essay with only details. It doesn't matter if you know all the nations who participate in the United Nations, for example. If you don't know the principles of the organization itself, you can't write a strong essay about it.

Objective tests can cover concept and detail, both for recall and recognition. Sometimes detail is more critical. Matching writers with their famous characters tests detail. Matching writers with the kind of literature they wrote tests concept.

Fill-in and short-answer items test recall. Multiple-choice and matching items test recognition. Recognition is easier for your memory than recall. But don't think a test will be easier if you find out it will have only multiple-choice and matching items. Items that test recognition can cover small details that the teacher wouldn't expect of you on a test for recall. You'll probably have to relearn more details for objective tests.

Sort and Organize. Sort through your materials and organize them. As you organize, put aside what you need to relearn.

Memorize the Difficult. Memorize any details or concepts that you've forgotten. Then put them with the material you remember.

Overlearn. Now go through everything. Don't be surprised if you find materials that need more work. Practice over and over again. Never be sure you have memorized anything perfectly.

Reorganize. Use cue trees, outlines, or other memory aids to reorganize the concepts from all of the material. If you can't clearly state what links the concepts together, go back and find the links.

Brainstorm. If you are facing a test, brainstorm questions that the teacher could ask. If your notes and other materials are thorough and organized, you know that the answers to any questions have to be there.

If you can't recall answers to some of your own questions, devise more memory aids. For example, when preparing for an essay test, think of some questions that will likely be asked. Sometimes your teacher will even tell you the topics. Find the concepts and details you want to use to answer each question. Reduce each concept to one word only. Make an acronym of the words' first letters. Get suitable memory aids together for the details.

At the test, first write down your memory aids for the questions you anticipated. Then read through the test. If you've done a good job of organizing, even if you anticipated the wrong questions, you will have enough memory aids to do well.

IV MEMORIZING SPELLING

Several aids for improving your memory for spelling are given in this section.

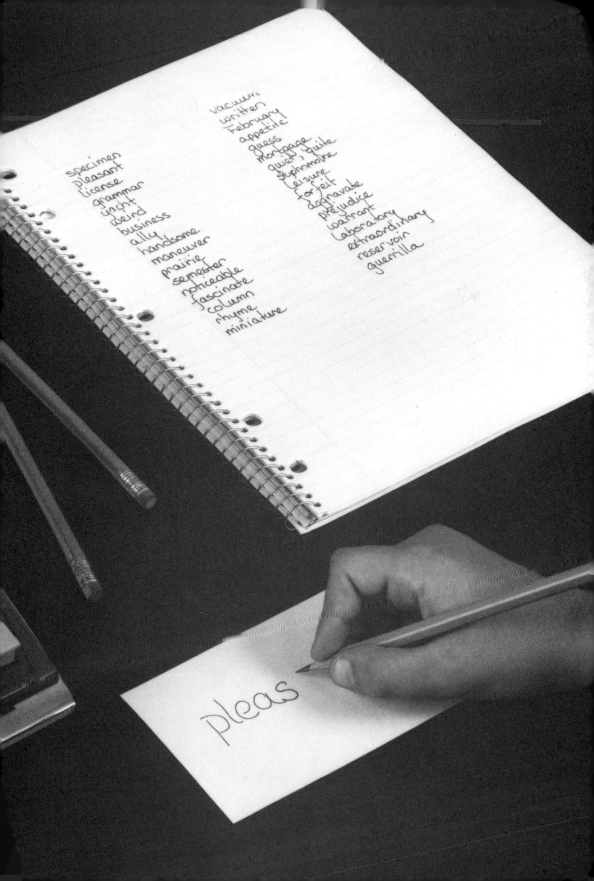

Memorizing Spelling

*M**any memory wizards can talk backward. If you say* backward *to them, they can say* drawkcab *instantly. One wizard could rattle off whole sentences backward, up to nine words. One wonders how much trouble this person would have had with*

Llanfairpwllgwyngyllgogerychwyrndrobwllllantysiliogogogoch

The name of this town in Wales has 58 letters.

There are probably about a million words in English today, spelled with twenty-six letters. How can you be expected to remember all those letter combinations, especially when many of the words follow no rules?

You memorize spellings one by one, as you need them. How you go about memorizing them will depend on a number of factors.

Often, classes conduct spelldowns, where students spell words aloud. While spelldowns can be fun, they aren't as effective as writing. Keep in mind that writing is the only situation in which spelling can possibly matter. So plan to write when memorizing spelling.

Aids for Spellers

If you are already a good speller, you probably don't need any special memory aids. They would waste your time. Many people have no problem spelling words just by sight.

If you spell well enough, but a few words baffle you, you might use an aid for those. You need to keep a list of words you have trouble with. If you don't have one now, start one.

If you are a poor speller, you are going to have to concentrate hard to memorize words. There are some tricks you can use, but you also need help from your teacher and perhaps your counselor. Read about the aids here, but be careful in adopting them. If you use too many, they might confuse you more than they help you.

Key Strategy

A key strategy in memorizing spelling is to have a good plan. Here are ten common steps good spellers use to memorize new words. See if you can adapt them to memorize spelling:

1. Look at the word and concentrate.
2. Copy the word. While copying doesn't help with most other memory tasks, it is critical in spelling.
3. Close your eyes and try to picture how the word looks.
4. Ask your teacher, a friend, or a family member how the word is pronounced. Listen carefully to the pronunciation.
5. Pronounce the word yourself until you get it right.
6. Divide the word into syllables. Look them up in a dictionary, if necessary. Pronounce the word, overemphasizing the syllables.
7. Say the letters of the word in order.
8. Rewrite the word.
9. Study difficult parts of the word.
10. Use the word in a familiar sentence.

After you have memorized the word's spelling, use the word as often as possible in writing. This will fix the spelling in your memory.

Special Spelling Aids

Here are two groups of special spelling aids: those to use for memorizing any word and those to use for word types, such as contractions or compounds.

For Any Word

Spelling Rules and Rhymes

There is a problem with spelling rules. They have many exceptions. Memorizing the rules and all their exceptions would be a real challenge.

Why not limit yourself to the rules and exceptions that are giving you trouble? Once you have a list of words you often misspell, you can match them up to the spelling rules. You don't have to memorize the rules you have no misspellings for. Memorize only those for which you do.

One easy-to-remember rule has a rhyme associated with it: *"I* before *e* except after *c,* or when sounded as *a,* as in *neighbor* and *weigh."* The rhyme makes the rule and its exceptions easy to memorize.

You might try creating your own rhymes for spelling rules and their exceptions. Here are two examples:

For words like *panic, panicky*:
Insert *k* after *c* with an *e,i,* or *y,*
But *arced* puts the *e* after *c*—don't ask why.
(There's usually no reason.)

For words like *admirable, admirably*:
Admirable ends with the silent vowel *e.*
Drop the *e* when you add a vowel—admirably.
This rule's a good tool, but it's been known to budge.
A familiar exception is the word *mileage.*

The time you invest in creating rhymes like these will probably enable you to remember spelling rules and exceptions you're having trouble with.

Emphasizing the Error

If rewriting a word you misspell doesn't help you, try rewriting it a different way. Emphasize the errors you are making.

If you consistently misspell *hangar* as *hanger,* for example, write the misspelling a few times, making the *e* a capital letter: *hangEr.* Cross the *E* out each time in black.

Then write the word correctly a few times, capitalizing the second *a: hangAr.* Circle the *A* each time in red.

Word Associations

Some people can improve their spelling by associating the words that give them trouble with other words. If you leave the *t* out of *fasten,* think "fasten ten tentacles." *Freight* can be a hard word to spell, but most of us remember *eight.* Think "eight freight cars." This aid helps you remember by isolating the area where the misspelling occurs.

"Ho, ho, ho, ho."

Mental Pictures

Mental pictures are good aids for memorizing spelling. Say you can't remember to put the *h* in *ghost.* Picture a ghost saying "Ho, ho, ho." If you can't remember to put two *o*'s in *chocolate,* picture the word with two tomatoes in place of the *o*'s.

Capitalization is a part of spelling. Mental pictures can help you memorize capitalizations. Suppose you want to remember that *Roman* in *Roman numerals* is capitalized. Picture a giant wearing a toga. The giant cues the capital letter. For *dutch oven,* picture a dutch oven with a ladle over it. The ladle's bowl should be to the left, forming the small letter *d.*

Alphapegs

You can use alphapegs with mental pictures to help you avoid misspellings. If you misspell *appetite* as *appatite,* for example, always picture a stomach with an eel wrapped around it to cue the *e* in the correct spelling. For *grammar* rather than *grammer,* think of a grandmother with an ant over her head to cue the *a.*

Acrostics

Making up catchy acrostics from the first letters of words you misspell can also help you memorize them. If you can't remember how to spell *arithmetic,* try it this way:

A rat in the house might eat the ice cream.

The first letter of each of these words spells *arithmetic.* Or, for *weird:*

Witches eat in rattraps daily.

Clustering

Sometimes you'll find that clustering exceptions to spelling rules is the best way to memorize them. One spelling rule is to double the final consonant before a suffix beginning with a vowel: *sadden, repelled, occurred.* Exceptions are *crocheting, ricocheted.*

If you can't remember these two words by rote, remember them as a pair. You can also make up a sentence with both words in it. Remember the sentence anytime you have to use either of the words. Your sentence can make sense like "The crocheting woman's hook flew out of her hand and ricocheted off the wall" or it can be nonsense like "The crocheting crocodile's hook ricocheted off the tent and dumped the tea."

Daffynitions

Sometimes odd definitions with or without mental pictures can help you remember how to spell. *Accidentally,* for example, is an accident with an ally (*accident* + *ally*). *Pageant* is a page with an ant crawling on it (*page* + *ant*).

Taping Mispronunciations

Do you say *athalete* for *athlete*? *excape* for *escape*? *stoled* for *stole*? If so, you might be misspelling these words. Mispronunciation often causes spelling errors.

If you consistently misspell the same words, check their pronunciations in a dictionary. If you have been mispronouncing any of the words, cluster them in a simple list and have them taped. Listening to correct pronunciations might achieve what seeing the words correctly spelled hasn't.

Have your teacher or a family member do the taping so you're sure the pronunciation is correct. You might want to place a word like *stole* in a sentence, since *stoled* is a spelling error caused partly by misusage ("Yesterday he stole the car," not "Yesterday he stoled the car").

Play back the first word. Listen carefully, pronounce it, and write it. Repeat until you have written the word correctly several times. Then go on to the next word.

When you have finished, read the words back aloud, checking your pronunciation against the tape. Repeat the entire exercise at intervals, perhaps every two days, until you are sure you have memorized all the pronunciations and spellings.

For Word Types

You can organize words into types that give you spelling problems. One type is contractions, like *aren't* or *can't*. Another is compound words, which consist of combinations of words, their combining forms, and prefixes and suffixes. Examples are *metallike, dislike,* and *likable.*

Confusing two or more words sometimes causes you to misspell. We confuse homophones, for example, which are words that sound identical but have different meanings and spellings. Examples are *brake* and *break, idle* and *idol.* Other confusing words look almost alike, such as *angel* and *angle, trail* and *trial.*

Here are some strategies for memorizing words by type and strategies for spelling words that are "a foot and a half long."

Contractions

We're always looking for ways to shorten what we're saying. People've always done so. Because we've shortened so many words, many contractions've sneaked into our written language. If we'd known they'd cause spelling problems, we mightn't have let'em. But you've got to memorize'em, and their spellings aren't always easy.

Here are some common contractions found in writing and the words they come from:

aren't	are not
can't	cannot
didn't	did not
doesn't	does not
don't	do not
hadn't	had not
hasn't	has not
haven't	have not
he'll	he will
he'd	he had/would
he's	he is/has
I'd	I had/would
I'll	I shall/will
I'm	I am
isn't	is not
it'll	it will
it's	it has/is
I've	I have
let's	let us
mustn't	must not
she'll	she will
shouldn't	should not
that's	that is
there's	there is
they're	they are
what's	what is
who's	who is
won't	will not
you'd	you had/would
you're	you are
you've	you have

Memorize contractions in three easy steps. First, remember that one apostrophe belongs in the contraction somewhere. (Students shouldn't use contractions with more than one apostrophe in writing.) Second, remember that the contraction itself is one word—no spaces. And last, if you have any doubts about how a contraction is spelled, say or write it in full form.

If you're having trouble with *didn't,* say *did not.* Put the apostrophe where the missing letter, *o,* is, and spell the rest of the contraction the same way as in the full form, joining the two words.

Some contractions are missing more than one letter (*he'll, he'd*), but the same principle holds. Be careful with *can't*—you cannot hear that one *n* dropped.

As always, there are some special problems. *Won't* (*will not*) is irregularly spelled. But it sounds the same as it's spelled. Just put the apostrophe where the *o* in *not* would be.

Bigger problems come with contractions that sound like other words (*it's/its, there's/theirs, they're/their/there, who's/whose*). Again your best strategy is to say the word in full form. If you can split the word into two different words and your sentence still makes sense, then you have a contraction:

> Who's here? → Who is here?
> Whose coat is that? → Who is coat is that? (Nonsense.)
> I think they're here. → I think they are here.
> I think there are more. → I think there are are more. (Nonsense)

Compound Words

The spellings of many compound words are easy because they are just a joining of two common words, with no letters changed:

catfish
housecoat
outlast
sandbox

Other compound words add prefixes and suffixes. Many of these words are rather easy to spell:

ashore (prefix *a-*)
untie (prefix *un-*)
bakery (suffix *-y*)
walking (suffix *-ing*)

Spelling problems occur when letters drop out of compound words:

already (not *allready*)
pastime (not *passtime*)

Sometimes adding a prefix or suffix makes a word look unusual, so people misspell it:

extra- + ordinary = extraordinary
                    (not *extrordinary*)
mis- + spell =   misspell (not *mispell*)
approximate + -ly = approximately
                    (not *approximatly*)
ski + -ing =   skiing (not *sking*)

Prefixes and suffixes can also be attached to root words, which you might not recognize standing alone. The root's spelling can vary, depending on what's attached to it:

extend, extent (*tend* or *tent* = *to tend* or *stretch*) triangle, triangular (*angle* or *angul* = *corner*)

There are spelling rules that tell how to deal with compound words that we frequently misspell. But, as you know, there are many exceptions to those rules. So your best aid for memorizing compound words is first to be aware of what they are and the kinds of problems they cause. Then review their spelling rules and keep track of the compound words that are problems for you.

When you come across a troublemaker, list it with your other misspelled words and follow the key strategy at the beginning of this section. For words like *approxi-*

mately, concentrate especially on overemphasizing the syllables:

ap / prox / i / mate / ly

If the key strategy doesn't help, you might be able to memorize a compound word by using other aids. To memorize
the spelling of *skiing,* for example, picture a ski on one
side of a brick wall and an inkwell on the other side. The
brick wall will suggest a division between the two word
parts.

    If you're putting an extra *s* in *pastime,* emphasize the
error by writing the word and crossing the extra *s* out, then
writing the word correctly and circling the single *s.*

    Make up a sentence for *extraordinary:* "Extra olives
make extra oil." This should cue you that an *o* follows the
a in *extra.*

Confused Words

Words That Sound Alike. If you are having trouble spelling homophones, memorize their spellings in pairs. Here are some examples of homophones:

brake/break
idle/idol
pedal/peddle
steal/steel

Write two sentences on each side of a flashcard. One sentence describes one of the homophones. The other sentence uses the other homophone to cue the first one. You have to spell the homophone to fit the description. For example:

Side 1

It stops a car. It sounds like *break*.
(Spell *brake*.)

Side 2

It splits in two. It sounds like *brake*.
(Spell *break*.)

You can also put synonyms for both homophones on one side of a flashcard and the homophones on the other. Then name and spell the homophone for each synonym:

Side 1	Side 2
lazy	idle
hero	idol

Words That Look Almost Alike. Here are some words that are so close in spelling, people often confuse them:

angel, angle
trail, trial
which, witch

If you are having trouble spelling words that look almost alike, memorize their spellings together. You can use either of the aids for homophones. In the first example, change the sentence to "It looks somewhat like. . . . "

Or you can use mental pictures. For *angel,* picture an angel with an elephant on a leash, trailing behind. The *el* in *elephant* will cue the *el* at the end of *angel.* For *angle,* picture a leprechaun wearing angles for shoes.

Sesquipedalians

One long English word in the dictionary has 45 letters:

pneumonoultramicroscopicsilicovolcanoconiosis

It's the name of a dangerous lung disease that afflicts miners. You might think this word is hard to spell, but it's not—if you split it into meaningful units to analyze:

pneumono / ultra / micro / scopic / silico / volcano / con / iosis

The units really leap out at you when you isolate them. That's the key to spelling long words—recognizing their units. The units also help you pronounce and understand the word.

You probably already know how to spell *ultra, micro, scopic,* and *volcano.* All you have left is *pneumono,* which is similar to *pneumonia; silico,* which with an *n* would be *silicon; con,* which you spell all the time (as in *consent* or *content*); and *iosis,* a common medical ending that you might recognize.

Word analysis is a common strategy for memorizing spellings and meanings for both ordinary and sesquipedalian, or long, words. The word *sesquipedalian* itself is long. It means *a foot and a half long,* from Latin *sesqui, one and one half,* and *ped,* or *foot.* That leaves *-alian,* as in *Episcopalian.* Let's look at some more sesquipedalian words:

antidisestablishmentarianism
hemidemisemiquaver
magnetohydrodynamics
sesquicentennial
triskaidekaphobia

With the help of your dictionary, analyze these words and memorize how to pronounce and spell them. If you do, you should have no problem doing the same with words only half their length.

V MEMORIZING VOCABULARY

This section shows how to memorize vocabulary through a number of aids you can use along with your dictionary.

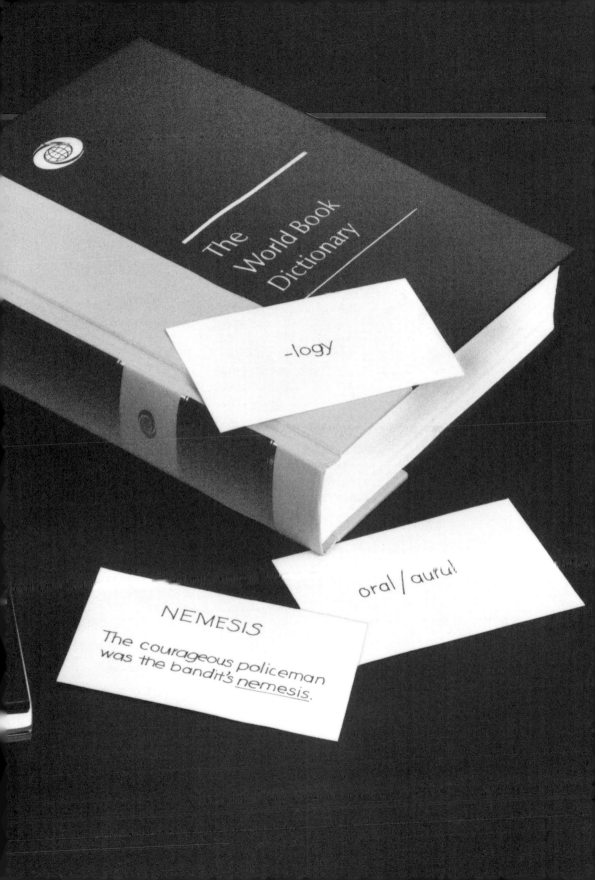

Memorizing Vocabulary

*M*emory wizards aren't necessarily brilliant. One store clerk had an IQ of 136—over the average, but not uncommon. Yet this wizard had a reading knowledge of all the modern European languages except Greek and Hungarian. To name some, that means Albanian, Czech, English, Finnish, French, German, Italian, Norwegian, Polish, Portuguese, Romanian, Russian, and Spanish. It seems impossible that anyone could read and understand all those languages.

The average American has an active (recall) vocabulary for speaking and writing of about 10,000 words, with a reading and understanding (recognition) vocabulary of 30,000 to 40,000 words. Our memory wizard's recognition vocabulary was many times 40,000 words. How is such a skill developed? By starting with a base of words, just like yours.

Words have much in common, both within and among languages. *Absolute,* in English, for example, is *absolut* in French, *absolut* in German, and *absoluto* in Spanish. Terms that look similar in different languages might have somewhat different uses, but people can often make sense of them in the context of a conversation or reading passage.

You have a base of English words that will help you, through association, to memorize other English words. With every new word you memorize, you will build another cue on which to fasten yet more words and understandings.

Take *command* and *demand.* You know that they both mean *to order.* This understanding should lead you to know that the words *mandate* and *mandatory* also have something to do with orders. The words have a root word for order: *mand.* That's your first cue in memorizing *mandate* and *mandatory.* If you look them up in the dictionary, you'll find more cues. Look them up now.

The dictionary is an important source for memorizing vocabulary. Its aids include a word's pronunciation, origin, definitions, parts of speech, synonyms, antonyms, and sentence examples.

But sometimes the dictionary isn't enough. This section will help you memorize vocabulary through a number of aids you can use along with your dictionary.

Senses and Direct Experience

Preschool children memorize most of their words through the senses via direct experience. They see, hear, touch, taste, and smell things, hear the words for them during the experience, and eventually bring the words into their vocabularies.

Older people can memorize words in much the same way. If you bite into a rotten nut and someone says it must taste putrid, you'll remember that *putrid* means *rotten* or *decayed* partly through your sense of taste. If you're in a field of flowers and someone says they are aromatic, you'll remember that *aromatic* means *good smelling* partly through your sense of smell.

Direct experience builds vocabulary. If you want to remember the word *perforate,* punch a piece of paper through with a pencil. Look at the hole that's left and feel it. Your senses of touch and sight will help you remember what *perforate* means. If you want to remember what a *fugue* is, listen to one (it's a kind of musical composition). Your sense of hearing will fix the memory of *fugue*'s meaning in your mind.

Recording

To take advantage of your excellent ability to memorize what you hear, tape and play back your memory aids for vocabulary. The aids can include definitions, familiar sentences, rhymes, and other aids you will learn about later in this section. Your ears will give your eyes a boost.

Rote

Some people can memorize definitions simply by rote. If you can remember, for example, that *alacrity* means *brisk and eager action* by just reading the definition, do so. Add a familiar sentence that uses the word: *The spry old man walked with alacrity.* Never leave the sentence out. You'll remember the word more easily if you can use it in a familiar context.

Flashcards can help you memorize by rote. Put the word on one side with a sentence that uses the word and put the definition on the other. Practice back and forth. First read the word and sentence and recall the definition. Then read the definition and recall the word and sentence.

Flashcards can help you memorize by rote.

Rhyme

Ogden Nash wrote:

> The cow is of the bovine ilk;
> One end is moo, the other milk.

Anyone who has ever read that verse can testify to the ability of rhyme to make us remember words. *Bovine* is something of, relating to, or resembling a cow or ox.

Try your own hand at rhyme to memorize vocabulary definitions. Your verses might not be brilliant, but only you will know them. Memory aids are personal matters.

You can make up a verse for each of your vocabulary terms, or combine them. Here are examples of verses that combine *tedious* and *drones, excavate* and *hovels,* and *pathetic, excess,* and *debilitate:*

> Tedious is as tedious does.
> Tedious drones, like hum and buzz.

> To excavate, take picks and shovels.
> Dig up bones from ancient hovels.

> Pathetic, such a sad estate,
> In excess will debilitate.

Redefining

You've learned that putting a word in the context of a familiar sentence helps you to memorize its meaning. Definitions are also easier to remember when the language is familiar to you.

Always redefine your vocabulary words after you look them up in the dictionary. Here are several ways to redefine words. Pick the best way for any word you are trying to remember:

Formal definition
A direct statement that defines the word for you.

Disarmament means reducing armies and navies and their equipment.

Definition by synonym
Defines the word with one of its synonyms.

Incessant means nonstop.

Definition by example
Includes an example to help you understand the definition.

Alliteration means repeating the first sound or the same first letter in a group of words: The *s*un sank *s*lowly.

Definition by description
Describes the word in a picture.

Erosion means wearing away the earth. Running water carries sand, gravel, and boulders and then deposits them somewhere else.

Definition by comparison
Compares something directly to something else.

A *dromedary* is a camel with one hump and short hair.

Definition by simile
Compares something to something else using *like* or *as*.

A *love seat* is like a small sofa.

Definition by contrast Compares something to something else and also shows its difference.	A *farce* is like a comedy but it is silly, not just amusing.
Definition by appositive Identifies a noun in a sentence; commas set off the appositive.	*Schussing,* skiing straight down a slope without turning or stopping, is the fastest form of skiing.
Definition by origin Defines a word in terms of its origin.	*Nectar* comes from the ancient Greek word for the drink of the gods.
Parenthetical definition Includes a definition in parentheses.	An important part of character is *integrity* (good values).
Indirect definition Defines a word indirectly using words such as *called, also called, or, known as, referred to,* and *that is.*	Cameras control the amount of light passing through a lens with changeable openings, also called *stops.*

Word Play

When memorizing vocabulary, be creative. Play with the words.

When memorizing vocabulary, be creative. Play with the words. Suppose you are having trouble remembering the figures of speech. Use cues from the words themselves— rhyme, alliteration—to make the definitions come back more easily. For example, to remember the meaning of the word *metaphor,* you might make up a sentence such as:

> Metaphors mentally force you to compare two things through a symbol.

There is alliteration in the *m-t-f* sounds and the phrase "mentally force" also sounds like *metaphor.* Don't forget to add a sentence with a metaphor: Dad's a pearl.

Or, to memorize the word *allegory,* you might say:

> An allegory is a story full of metaphors. The symbols are just more.

This definition not only rhymes but also builds on the last definition. Then think of a sentence with an example: "The Hare and the Tortoise," one of Aesop's fables, is an allegory.

Mental and Other Pictures

Because mental pictures are good memory joggers, you can add them to your definitions. For *metaphor*, picture a mosquito with a hypodermic needle. For *circumference*, picture a circle with a ring of circus elephants around it.

Sometimes your textbooks provide pictures in the form of graphs, charts, diagrams, and maps. For social studies, if you are trying to memorize what inflation means, a graph of U.S. inflation for the last twenty years might appear. It will show how prices have increased over that time period.

Inflation happens when a government increases the amount of paper money it issues. The more paper money available, the less it's worth, and the more of it you need to buy anything. So prices rise.

That's a lot to remember. Help yourself by memorizing the graph. It will be a cue to the definition for the word *inflation* because the graph line shows prices going up. (You can also remember what inflation is by picturing yourself at the cash register handing over a bunch of shrunken dollars in exchange for a doughnut.)

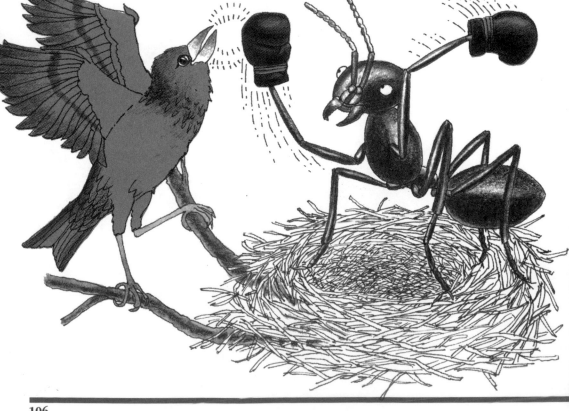

Key Words

So far in this discussion, you have already seen some key words used to help memorize vocabulary. Did you recognize them? If not, go back. Then let's look at some more.

To remember what *congestion* (concentrated in a small space) means, see *gorilla chests + jungle*—a mass of gorilla chests crammed into a jungle. To remember *antagonist* (an opponent), see *ant + on + nest*—an ant with boxing gloves standing on a bird's nest, punching the bird. Now think up some of your own for *disheveled, harbinger,* and *minuscule.* Look them up first in the dictionary if you have to.

Acronyms

For memorizing short vocabulary terms, you can use the terms themselves as acronyms of their definitions.

CHAOS = *C*onfusion *h*as *a*bsolutely *o*vertaken *s*ociety.

GAUNT = *G*ot *a*n *u*nfed, *n*ubby *t*orso.

See if you can develop definitions this way for *flout* and *jaunt.*

You can also create acronyms that don't tie in with a vocabulary word's spelling. But they relate to the word indirectly through spelling, pronunciation, or meaning, and have the letters of a good definition.

antidote = COPE—*c*ontrols *o*ne's *p*oison *e*ffectively

rhapsody = ROPE—*r*ecitation *o*f *p*oem, *e*pic

Find acronyms and develop definitions for *allusion* and *specter* this way.

Word Parts

You learned in Section IV that you can use word parts to remember how to spell. You can also use them to remember definitions.

Prefixes, Suffixes, and Roots

Rote

You need to memorize prefixes, suffixes, and roots in order to use them as memory joggers.

You need to memorize prefixes, suffixes, and roots in order to use them as memory joggers. Some will be easy to remember because they are in words you know that give clues. Memorize these word parts by rote, with flashcards as needed. Here are some examples:

Prefix	Suffix	Root
anti-	*-graph*	*aqua*
(against:	(writing:	(water:
antiseptic)	autograph)	aquarium)
re-	*-ist*	*circ*
(again:	(person who:	(ring:
reread)	dentist)	circle)
sub-	*-ward*	*flex*
(under:	(direction:	(bend:
submarine)	backward)	flexible)

When using flashcards, put the word parts on the front and the meanings on the reverse. Go back and forth through the cards until you are sure you have memorized the parts. If you have chosen truly easy word parts for rote memorization, you shouldn't need any words that contain the parts on the flashcards.

Meaning Clusters

Putting things in clusters, or categories, makes them easier to remember. You've already clustered easy word parts by selecting to memorize their meanings by rote.

Memorize some of the word parts you find more difficult by placing them in clusters according to meaning.

"Not" Prefixes	"State of" Suffixes	"Move" Roots
a-	*-ance*	*migr*
(anemia)	(annoyance)	(migration)
im-	*-dom*	*mot*
(immovable)	(kingdom)	(motor)
ir-	*-ism*	*ag*
(irritable)	(hypnotism)	(agitate)

Use flashcards again, this time putting the cluster of word parts on one side and their meaning on the other.

Word Clusters

You can memorize word parts by clustering words that have them. Here are some examples:

Prefix *pan-*, "all"	Suffix *-ide*, "kill"	Root *mime*, "imitate"
Pan-American	algaecide	mime
pandemic	fungicide	mimeograph
pandemonium	germicide	mimic
panorama	suicide	pantomime

This time, put the word clusters on one side of the flashcard with the word part at the top. On the back, put the word part's meaning.

During tests and at other times when you can't get to a dictionary, make sure to brainstorm words with the same word parts as words whose meanings you can't remember. The brainstormed words might jog your memory. This is how your thoughts should flow:

impartial	*Partial* means preferring something. *Immovable* means not movable. *Impartial* means not partial to someone or something.
herbicide	An *herb* is a plant. *Suicide* means to kill oneself. An *herbicide* kills plants.

spectrometer The *spectrum* has many colors. A *metric table* contains measures. A *spectrometer* measures color.

More Key Words

You can use key words to memorize word parts. For the prefix *ambi-,* think of a two-headed Bambi (*ambi-* means *two*). For the suffix *-logy,* think of a lodge in a test tube (*-logy,* pronounced like "lodgey," means *science*). For the root *hum,* think of a hummingbird hopping on a pile of dirt (*hum* means *earth, soil*). Can you think of some key words for *macro-* (*long*), *-icle* (*little*), and *densus* (*thick*)?

Base Words

English has about 3,000 base words that take care of 95 per cent of anyone's communication needs. An example is *like*. From this base word, we can build *likes, liked, liken, liking; likability, likable, likelihood, likeliness, like-minded, likeness, likewise; unlike, unliked, unliking, unlikable, unlikely; childlike, starlike, and wormlike.*

Look for base words when memorizing your vocabulary. Here are some words whose meanings are easy to memorize because of their base words:

demoniac   like a demon (devilish, fiendish)

elephantine   like an elephant (heavy, clumsy)

statuesque   like a statue (graceful, dignified)

Can you figure out the meanings of *porcine* and *textual* on your own?

Literature and Base Words

Some words come from the names of literary places or characters. Look for either in your vocabulary terms. Here are some examples:

Armageddon	From the Bible's description of the final great battle between good and evil. Any great and final conflict.
eden	From the Bible's Garden of Eden. A paradise.
nemesis	From Nemesis, the Greek goddess of revenge. Any person or thing that justly punishes someone else for evil deeds.
plutocracy	From Pluto, Greek king of the underworld, where the world's riches were believed to be stored. A government ruled by the wealthy.

Can you figure out the meanings for *goliath* (from the Bible's David and Goliath) and *mercurial* (from the Roman messenger god, Mercury)?

Foreign Terms

You can use base words to memorize the meanings of foreign terms adapted into English. Here are some French words used in English whose meanings are easy to remember because parts of the words resemble English words:

facade   Think *face*. A facade is the front of a building.

protégé   Think *protected*. A protégé is someone protected by someone else.

raconteur   Think *recount*. A raconteur is a storyteller.

Can you figure out the meanings of *attaché* and *nouveau riche* on your own?

Context Clues and Memorization

Any time you come across a word you don't know in a reading selection, take note to memorize it.

Any time you come across a word you don't know in a reading selection, take note to memorize it. You might be able to do so without looking it up if you notice the word's associations with ideas and other words in the selection. Here's an example:

> Teeth are the hardest tissues of the human body. A tooth consists of a crown, an underlying dentin, and a soft pulp.

A dictionary definition might be:

> a calcereous material forming the main tooth mass, like but harder and denser than bone, that composes the principal mass of a tooth.

That's a mouthful. From the passage you could have made up the following definition, without ever looking in the dictionary:

> Dentin is the hard middle part of a tooth.

That's probably all you need. See if you can figure out what *caldera* means from this sentence:

> The volcano's caldronlike caldera was spitting fire and molten rock.

Pairing Words

Your memory might get a boost if you pair words to memorize their definitions. You can, for example, pair synonyms, antonyms, and confused words.

Synonym and Antonym Pairs

If you can find a one-word equivalent for a word's meaning or its opposite, memorize the two as a synonym or antonym pair. Use flashcards for each set, putting one word on each side. Here are some examples:

Synonyms	Antonyms
anomalous/odd	anomalous/normal
destitute/poor	destitute/rich
perpetrate/commit	perpetrate/prevent
prolong/lengthen	prolong/shorten
zealous/eager	zealous/reluctant

Confused Words

You can also use flashcards to memorize the meanings of words you confuse. Start a list of them. When you have a few, write each pair on the front of a flashcard and the definitions for both on the back. Use synonyms whenever you can to keep the definitions short.

Here are some examples of confused-word pairs:

Confused Pair	Definitions
aerie/eerie	eagle's nest/strange
accept/except	take/but
affect/effect	influence/outcome

bland/blend	tasteless/mix
loath/loathe	reluctant/hate
scow/scowl	boat/frown

It's effective to use familiar sentences when memorizing word pairs whose usages confuse you. For *accept* and *except,* add this to the card:

> I accept your gift. / I can do nothing except accept your gift.

What sentences would you write for *affect/effect* and *loath/loathe?*

Putting Yourself in the Picture

A last aid for memorizing vocabulary depends on your creativity in picturing yourself as part of a definition. You did this earlier in a small way to remember what *inflation* means by picturing yourself handing over shrunken dollars to pay for a doughnut.

Put yourself prominently in the picture when you memorize the meanings of scientific terms for physical processes. You'll find that you yourself are an excellent memory aid.

Let's start with *refraction.* The dictionary tells us that refraction is:

> the process of turning or bending a ray of light when it passes at an angle from one medium into another of different density.

Say it in simple terms:

> A ray of light slants down through the air, hits something, and bends.

Now imagine yourself as a ray of light slanting down from the sky and hitting a wall. You'll bend, and no doubt get a fracture.

Another example is *osmosis*, which the dictionary says is:

> the tendency of two fluids of different strengths that are separated by something porous to go through it and become mixed.

Say it in simple terms:

> Two uneven fluids tend to mix evenly when they're separated by something that has pores because the fluids can pass through it.

Imagine yourself filled with green water. Jump into a vat of clear water. The water in the vat and the water in you will mix into the same shade of green as the two fluids pass back and forth through your skin (which has pores).

Now try to put yourself into the meanings of *dispersion* and *reflection*. Don't forget to reword the definitions first.

VI

UNBLOCKING YOUR MEMORY

This section explains how your memory gets blocked, and it gives simple methods and aids for clearing up blocked memory.

Unblocking Your Memory

S tudents can develop a sort of forgetfulness like amnesia when they are being evaluated at school, especially during tests. It's not real amnesia, which is a clinical condition that can be serious. Students' forgetfulness is just a temporary memory block, often due to stress. Memory often comes right back after the test (to the student's dismay).

Ali Lameda, a Venezuelan poet imprisoned in North Korea for six years starting in 1967, knew how to overcome stress. He memorized 400 poems and 300 sonnets during that time. He is a memory wizard, and his accomplishment has meaning for you: you can overcome stress and other factors that may block your memory.

Reasons You Forget

There are four reasons why you forget: interference, retrieval failure, motivated forgetting, and constructive processes. Sometimes memory is never stored, even though you think it is. This isn't forgetting but, since it's related, it's discussed here, along with cramming, which can block your memory. At the end of this section, you will find out how you can avoid most school-related forgetting.

Interference

Interference happens when old memorized material blocks your memorization of new material, and vice versa. You can't, for example, keep track of the characters in the *Iliad* because you've just finished memorizing the characters in the *Odyssey*. Or you're having a test on coordinating conjunctions after you have begun to study subordinating conjunctions. You're getting them mixed up. Interference can be bothersome.

Retrieval Failure

Retrieval failure happens when you know you memorized something but you can't recall it, no matter how hard you concentrate. You can't, for example, remember the name for a negatively charged atomic particle (electron). Then the name comes back to you the moment you turn in your test. Your memory has failed you, and again you're disappointed.

Motivated Forgetting

Motivated forgetting is consciously or unconsciously wanting to forget something, and doing so. You haven't enjoyed studying perimeter formulas. You don't like math. When you get to the test, you can't remember the formulas, even though you're sure you memorized them. Such situations can cause frustration.

Constructive Processes

Constructive processes are involved when someone changes or makes up a memory and believes the new memory is true. A student shows this kind of forgetting when insisting to a teacher that an answer which was marked wrong is right. The student remembers seeing the answer in the textbook. When the student looks up the answer, the textbook proves the teacher is right.

No Memory Stored

Sometimes memory isn't stored at all, for one of three reasons. The stimulus didn't last long enough for your memory to store it. You didn't notice the stimulus, even though it did last long enough. Or you noticed the stimulus, but didn't pay enough attention to store it.

Think of a penny. It has eight main features: four on the front and four on the back. Can you remember them? Try, and then look at a penny to see how well you did. In one memory study, people tested were able to recall an average of only three of the eight features.

People don't remember many things they frequently see, although they might think their memory of these things is perfect. Memorizing takes interest and concentration. Frequently looking at your textbook and notes, for example, won't guarantee that you'll remember anything from them.

Be honest with yourself when you think your memory is fighting you. Did you memorize the forgotten information in the first place? If not, you have only yourself to blame.

Cramming

When you are facing a test the next day and know none of the material, cramming might be the only way you can hope to pass the test. But so far as remembering later goes, the time spent cramming is largely wasted.

When you cram, information doesn't sink deep into your memory. In fact, at the end of a cram session, when you're head is swimming with details, you are just about at the right point to begin memorizing to avoid block— through concepts and understanding.

Cramming is also hard work. When you're done, you are exhausted and nervous. Don't count on your memory to cooperate.

Aids to Blocked Memory

Many ways to unblock your memory involve common sense. Others involve understanding how your memory works and using aids you know will jog it.

Thorough Memorization

Thorough memorization takes time but prevents blocked memory.

Thorough memorization takes time but prevents blocked memory. The more you practice, the more solid your memory is. You recall information quicker and keep it longer. And your memory has a better chance of resisting stress, fatigue, and distractions.

Spaced Review

Your memories for schoolwork are going to fade and become somewhat confused with time. They are rarely completely lost if you memorized thoroughly to begin with, but the more time passes, the more likely your memory is to become fuzzy.

Spaced review will bring back your memory and fix it firmly so it doesn't block. Keep in mind that the total hours you spend memorizing the night before a test don't count. The total hours you spend in the weeks before do.

If you are reviewing two sets of material that are quite alike, memorize them in two different locations. This will help keep the material separated in your memory and prevent later interference problems at the test.

Allow some distractions now and then while you review. As a result, distractions will be less likely to block your memory when you need to use it.

Positive Attitude

At one time or another, all of us would rather forget something than remember it. After a test on punctuating main and dependent clauses, for example you might want to forget you ever saw a clause.

This kind of negativity does you a disservice on all sides. Your memorization might take longer because you are resisting the subject. And your negativity could make you block on a test, since you really still don't want to deal with the material.

The best attitude toward memorizing is a positive one. Decide that you really want to remember whatever you're working with. That's great insurance against your memory blocking.

Sleep

Sleep gives your memory a boost by lessening interference. As part of an experiment, some people were asked to go to sleep immediately after memorizing. Others in the group had to stay awake and do other activities. When later tested, the ones who went to sleep had better memories of what they had learned than did those who stayed awake. This suggests the influence sleep has on memory. Always get a good night's sleep before your memory has to perform, or you might suffer a block.

Relaxation

If you're stressed when trying to memorize, you can put the material aside until you calm down.

Worry, poor health, and poor diet can all cause stress. Stressed people often suffer poorer memory than those who are calm. Since stress can affect your memory, you should make it a policy to keep calm, healthy, and well nourished so that your memory is always in top form.

But even with this precaution, you will suffer stress from time to time. If you're stressed when trying to memorize, you can put the material aside until you calm down. But if you're stressed during a test, you have no way out. You might suffer a memory block.

We all have a peak memory point. It comes somewhere between waking up and the most stressful part of our day. This is why many students prefer to take tests in the morning, before they've built up to a stress point where their memory starts to decline.

You usually can't choose the time of a test. But you can choose to relax before it. Force yourself to forget about the material until you get to the test. If possible, try not to study or memorize anything else. Work out hard in P.E., talk with your friends, enjoy the day. If you allow tension to overcome you before the test, memory block night overcome you during it.

Memory Searching

No matter how many precautions you take, your memory will block from time to time. An excellent aid in this situation is memory searching.

Word Search

Say you have prepared a good rhyme cue for a social studies test on the French and Indian War. It contains the names of major conflicts plus some dates. When you get to the test, your memory blocks not only the rhyme, but almost everything from the lesson except the topic.

Forget the test questions for a few moments. Sit back and take deep breaths. Getting more oxygen in your system will help you relax. Break your thoughts for a moment by looking at what's going on outside the window. Then turn back to your work and start to free-associate any words that come to your mind when you think of war. Jot them down on the test sheet or on scratch paper.

Soon you will have a small group of words that start to jog other words from your memory. Start putting the words in logical order. Now look through the test for more memory cues. There should be some in the questions. With a little more searching, you should be able to remember what you memorized—including the memory aid that was blocked earlier.

Image Search

You might prefer to search your mind for images rather than words. Your memory is full of images besides the mental picture aids you develop for what you memorize.

If you're taking a geography test on earth's features, picture the earth. See mountains, valleys, peninsulas, deserts. Jot these down. They will call up the visuals in your textbook—pictures or diagrams of buttes, plains, mesas, shorelines. Note these too. Your image search will eventually unblock your memory.

First-Letter Search

For those times when you have a good grasp of concepts but can't come up with a detail, seek first-letter cues. This is a time-worn but excellent way to unblock your memory.

If you can't remember a name, for example, just go through the alphabet. You might come up with not only the name, but other information that was blocked.

Remember, in any memory situation, use what you have. There's no telling how far you can go with determination, a plan, and the many memory aids at your disposal

Index